HOLINESS IN NINETEENTH-CENTURY ENGLAND
The 1998 Didsbury Lectures

HOLINESS IN NINETEENTH-CENTURY ENGLAND
The 1998 Didsbury Lectures

David Bebbington

paternoster
press

Copyright © 2000 David Bebbington
First published in 2000 by Paternoster Press

06 05 04 03 02 01 00   7 6 5 4 3 2 1

Paternoster Press is an imprint of Paternoster Publishing,
P.O. Box 300, Carlisle, Cumbria, CA3 0QS, U.K.
Website: www.paternoster-publishing.com

British Library Cataloguing in Publication Data
A catalogue record for this book is available from the British Library

ISBN 0-85364-981-2

Cover Design by Mainstream, Lancaster
Typeset by WestKey Ltd, Falmouth, Cornwall
Printed in Great Britain by Bell & Bain Ltd, Glasgow

Contents

Preface

This book contains the Didsbury Lectures for 1998. They were in fact delivered at the Nazarene Theological College in Didsbury, Manchester, on four successive evenings in January 1999. Because the college stands in the Wesleyan theological tradition, laying particular emphasis on the attainability of holiness in this life, it seemed particularly appropriate to choose sanctification as the theme of the lectures. They are reproduced here in substantially the form in which they were delivered. For that reason they retain something of a rhetorical style, though critical apparatus and a list of recommended reading have been added.

I should like to thank the principal, Dr Herbert McGonigle, himself a historian of holiness, and the staff and members of the college for their invitation to give the lectures and for their warm hospitality during my stay. I should also like to express my gratitude to Dr Ian Randall of Spurgeon's College, London, for some references and for long-term help in understanding the spiritual traditions of Evangelicalism. My wife Eileen and daughter Anne, as so often, were indulgent during the intensive period of compiling the lectures; and Eileen gave wise advice about their content. I should like to dedicate the book to another member of my family, my aunt Madge Chave Jones. She has long been a resident of Manchester; she has for many years pursued the Christian life with dedication; and when I was young she gave me the history book that first opened my eyes to the fascinations of the past.

David Bebbington
Stirling
February 1999

Introduction

The theme of these chapters is holiness broadly conceived. It is a study of the quest for personal improvement in the Christian life. It covers aspects of personal piety, public devotion and their expression in action. All are set within a framework of theology, for that is how spirituality was understood and commended; all are also presented in their cultural context, for to leave that out would be to misrepresent reality. The treatment is necessarily selective, and consequently many aspects of religious experience are neglected here. Dreams and portents make no appearance, though they can be documented for the nineteenth century as for any other. The variation between types of spirituality based on gender, a subject that has recently been pioneered,[1] has been virtually omitted. And there is no coverage of one of the most salient features of piety in the period, the Christian deathbed, even though it figures largely in the sources.[2] Yet an attempt has been made to sketch some of the broad characteristics of holiness as understood in the nineteenth century.

There are further limitations on the range of material discussed here. The coverage is circumscribed, again for

---

[1] L. Wilson, 'Female Spirituality amongst Nonconformists, 1825–75', PhD dissertation, Cheltenham and Gloucester College of Higher Education, 1997.

[2] H. D. Rack, 'Evangelical Endings', *Bulletin of the John Rylands University Library of Manchester*, 74, 1992; P. Jalland, *Death in the Victorian Family*, Oxford, 1996.

reasons of space, by geography. Although much of what is said applies to the churches of Wales, Scotland and Ireland, and even to many of the churches of the farther-flung English-speaking world, the book confines itself to England. And it is by no means total in its consideration of the English churches. The chapters deal with several currents of opinion within the Church of England together with the mainstream Evangelical Nonconformists outside the Church of England. That leaves out not only the Roman Catholic Church but also tendencies within Anglicanism, notably Broad Church-manship, and a vast array of smaller denominations with their own distinctive piety – the Unitarians, the Churches of Christ, the Sandemanians and many others. It is particularly sad not to be able to include groups such as the Cokelers, a small sect that flourished in a few Sussex villages, who were teetotallers, pacifists, wore traditional smocks, ran a village store on the co-operative principle and officially taught the desirability of celibacy.[3] The denominational range is there-fore limited. Yet the traditions that are discussed must represent something like three-quarters of the churchgoers of the times. The book explores what were undoubtedly the main lines of spirituality in the Protestant churches.

The subject of holiness has attracted much more attention from historians of other periods in the history of the church. It is the central theme, for example, of a collection of essays on late antiquity by Peter Brown.[4] It is pivotal in the examination of the mediaeval monastic ethos in Jean Leclercq's *The Love of Learning and the Desire for God.*[5] Yet there has been a neglect of the topic in the recent past, from the eighteenth century to the present, especially in Britain. There has been more interest among historians in the subjects of the churches and society – the relation of religion to class – and of the churches and

---

[3] R. Homan, 'The Society of Dependents: A Case Study in the Rise and Fall of Rural Peculiars', *Sussex Archaeological Collections*, 119, 1981.

[4] P. Brown, *Society and the Holy in Late Antiquity*, London, 1982.

[5] J. Leclercq, *The Love of Learning and the Desire for God*, London, 1978.

politics – the relation of religion to power. The inward life, however, especially in the Evangelical tradition, has not received the attention it deserves. There are individual biographies that sometimes explore the personal spiritual life, but the patterns that affected the people en masse have been very little traced. The soul of the ordinary churchgoer has its own history waiting to be recorded.

There have been a number of indications that the era of neglect is passing. In Canada, for example, the late George Rawlyk has examined the spirituality of Henry Alline, the late eighteenth-century revivalist of Nova Scotia, in several works, and made Alline's style of enthusiastic piety the central organising principle of a broader thesis in *The Canada Fire*.[6] The United States has produced innovative works such as an exploration of African-American religious experience and a stimulating study of the material culture generated by spirituality.[7] In Britain there have been explorations of the Broad Churchmen, and especially Charles Kingsley, from the point of view of literary specialists; and recently there has appeared the path-breaking scrutiny of Roman Catholic devotion in Victorian England by Mary Heimann.[8] The existence of these works, in fact, more than compensates for the omission here of the Broad Church and Roman Catholic traditions. And they are symptoms of an incipient tendency to pay greater attention to questions in this broad field.

Yet the relative unfashionability of the areas that will be examined in these chapters does not mean that they have been totally neglected. In particular, the High Church tradition stemming from the Oxford Movement has for many years received its due. Pride of place in the considerable literature on

---

[6] G. Rawlyk, *The Canada Fire: Radical Evangelicalism in British North America, 1775–1812*, Kingston and Montreal, 1994.
[7] M. Sobel, *Trabelin' On: The Slave Journey to an Afro-Baptist Faith*, Princeton, N. J., 1988; C. McDannell, *Material Christianity: Religion and Popular Culture in America*, New Haven, Conn., 1995.
[8] N. Vance, *The Sinews of the Spirit*, Cambridge, 1985; M. Heimann, *Catholic Devotion in Victorian England*, Oxford, 1995.

Tractarian devotion must go to the work of Sir Owen Chadwick. His magisterial two-volume survey of *The Victorian Church* by no means ignores piety; his book *The Mind of the Oxford Movement* concentrates on devotional themes; and its main essay has more recently been reprinted with others in *The Spirit of the Oxford Movement*.[9] Partly as a result of Chadwick's oeuvre, the spirituality of the Oxford Movement is a regular feature of the standard accounts of nineteenth-century church history. Horton Davies, taking in all the main denominations, touches on the theme in his *Worship and Theology in England* volumes three and four, but, since his main concern is with liturgical matters, he necessarily allocates little space to private spirituality.[10] Raymond Brown's unpublished Cambridge doctoral dissertation on 'Evangelical Ideas of Perfection', tracing some of the main developments in the background of Keswick, is a pioneering exploration of the Evangelical side of the subject.[11] Though concentrating on periods other than the nineteenth century, Gordon Wakefield offers a helpful study of features of the Methodist tradition.[12] Melvin Dieter, in *The Holiness Revival of the Nineteenth Century*, is chiefly interested in America, but he does give space to the prelude to Keswick in Britain.[13] James Gordon's *Evangelical Spirituality* examines paired individuals from the eighteenth century to the present, and so illuminates something of the variety within Evangelicalism.[14] And Ian Randall has written on the

---

[9] O. Chadwick, *The Victorian Church*, London, 1966, 1970; id., *The Mind of the Oxford Movement*, London, 1960; id., *The Spirit of the Oxford Movement*, London, 1990.

[10] H. Davies, *Worship and Theology in England*, Princeton, N.J., vol. 3, *From Watts and Wesley to Maurice, 1690–1850*, 1961; vol. 4, *From Newman to Martineau, 1850–1900*, 1962.

[11] R. Brown, 'Evangelical Ideas of Perfection', PhD dissertation, University of Cambridge, 1965.

[12] G. S. Wakefield, *Methodist Devotion: The Spiritual Life in the Methodist Tradition*, London, 1966.

[13] M. Dieter, *The Holiness Revival of the Nineteenth Century*, Metuchen, N.J., 1980.

[14] J. M. Gordon, *Evangelical Spirituality*, London, 1991.

Evangelical movements of the inter-war period, so casting light on what went before.[15] These are all indications that the historical study of the soul is beginning to enjoy a greater vogue. With the growth of interest in contemporary spirituality, it may be expected that exploration of themes relating to holiness over the last three hundred years will increase during the twenty-first century.

The treatment of the subject here stresses the relationship of movements in spirituality to changes in the cultural setting. In a sense, these chapters form a case study of the complex bond between gospel and culture. They can be seen as an attempt, in the spirit of the writings of Lesslie Newbigin, to examine one of the ways in which the Christian faith has become embodied in Western civilisation.[16] The features of the setting that impinged most strikingly on the formulation of approaches to the spiritual life were the broad shifts in ideological mood that we label the Enlightenment and Romanticism. These phenomena were immensely diverse. The Enlightenment, for all its pretensions to rationality, had an undertow of fascination with the esoteric and even the occult; and Romanticism, for all its concern with imagining the past, had a hard-headed contemporary practicality about many of its artefacts, especially in the architectural sphere. Both movements of thought were very different over time and space. Yet their broad enduring qualities can be characterised, however imperfectly, in their main facets. It is generally recognised, for instance, that certain intellectual positions associated with the legacy of the Enlightenment and of Romanticism exercised a determining influence over the expressions of political thought during the nineteenth century. It is equally true that various motifs had a profound effect on the ways in which piety was conceptualised and practised. Holiness was intimately bound up with the spirit of the age.

---

[15] I. Randall, *Evangelical Experiences: A Study in the Spirituality of English Evangelicalism, 1918–1939*, Carlisle, 1999.

[16] L. Newbigin, *The Other Side of 1984: Questions for the Churches*, Geneva, 1983; id., *Foolishness to the Greeks: The Gospel and Western Culture*, London, 1986.

The traditions of spirituality selected for scrutiny here are four. The High Church mentality in the Church of England is the subject of the first chapter. The background in earlier forms of High Churchmanship is touched on, but the main weight falls on the transformation of Anglican devotion achieved by the Oxford Movement. In the second chapter, the theme is the approach to the Christian life nurtured by the Calvinist tradition in church and chapel alike. Again a contrast is drawn between earlier expressions of the tradition and the form that prevailed during the nineteenth century in the wake of the Evangelical Revival. The Wesleyan approach to piety, another fruit of the revival though largely confined to Methodism, is explored in the third chapter. After an examination of its broad characteristics, special attention is paid to the most distinctive element in the Wesleyan understanding, the experience of entire sanctification. The fourth chapter deals with the Keswick holiness movement that arose in the later Victorian years. There is discussion of its genesis, its particular features, and its debates with the two preceding traditions. The whole is rounded off with some overall conclusions about the significance of holiness in the nineteenth century.

Chapter One

The High Church Tradition

Developments in the High Church tradition of Anglicanism form the aspect of nineteenth-century spirituality that has been most extensively studied. It is virtually impossible to read an account of religion in Victorian England without encountering the Oxford Movement. That is one reason why High Churchmanship is a good place to begin an exploration of the century's piety. Another reason, however, is that the High Churchmen illustrate the predominant trends of the time most clearly. An analysis of their approach to the spiritual life lays bare some of the processes at work in society at large. They therefore constitute a useful reference point for the examination of the various Evangelical traditions that follows.

High Churchmanship was one of the long-standing tendencies within the Church of England. It was the tradition that laid the greatest weight on the doctrines of the church and the ministry and on the twin sacraments of baptism and communion. The key to High Churchmanship down the centuries is its insistence on ecclesiastical authority. The individual believer must submit his private judgement to that of the corporate church. The truth of its teaching is guaranteed by the apostolic succession, that is, the transmission of authority from the apostles to each successive generation of bishops. Episcopal rule is not just beneficial but absolutely essential to the church. Although the term High Church was first used to describe this understanding only in the late seventeenth century, the position it denotes had existed earlier: Archbishop Laud had embodied its attitudes under Charles I. During the eighteenth century, however, after the reign of Queen Anne, the party went into eclipse. Elevated claims for episcopal authority were associated with acceptance of the divine right of kings and with the exiled Jacobite claimants to the throne. The Hanoverian regime, from the reign of George I onwards, relegated such dangerous beliefs to the margins of national life. Nevertheless the tradition lived on – in Oxford, for this was the first of the lost causes for which the university became celebrated, and among some of the more tenacious of the clergy. Although the position could appear to be a relic of the past, it retained sufficient vigour to produce Samuel Horsley, Bishop of St Asaph from 1802 to 1806, and William Van Mildert, Bishop of Durham from 1826 to 1836. Both were men of intellectual standing and national significance.

The High Churchmen of the late eighteenth and early nineteenth centuries have recently been illuminated by Peter Nockles, one of the librarians at the John Rylands University of Manchester.[1] Nockles brings out the continuing vitality of High Churchmanship. The so-called 'Orthodox' party in the Church of England already held many of the convictions of the Oxford Movement long before it took its rise in the 1830s. The Orthodox, however, were distinguished from the later movement by retaining a stoutly Protestant stance. They were as anti-Catholic in their views as the Evangelicals, rejoicing in the Reformation and friendly to the continental Protestant churches. In the field of spirituality, they emphasised the importance of observing the patterns laid down by the church. Feelings in religion were not anathema, but there was a definite trend for High Churchmen to become more suspicious of them in the wake of the French Revolution and in reaction against the rising Evangelicals. Religious emotion seemed 'enthusiastic', something calculated to foster civil disorder and to carry off its devotees into non-establishment channels. The sober piety of late Georgian High Churchmanship around 1820 is evocatively described by the

---

[1] P. B. Nockles, *The Oxford Movement in Context: Anglican High Churchmanship, 1760–1857*, Cambridge, 1994.

novelist Charlotte M. Yonge in *Chantry House*, one of the best sources for appreciating the evolution of the tradition:

> My father and mother were both of the old-fashioned orthodox school, with minds formed on Jeremy Taylor, Blair, South, and Secker, who thought it their duty to go to church twice on Sunday, communicate four times a year (their only opportunities) after grave and serious preparation, read a sermon to their household on Sunday evenings, and watch over their children's religious instruction, though in a reserved and undemonstrative manner.[2]

The sources of influence, though including the near-contemporary Scottish model of eloquence Hugh Blair, were chiefly judicious divines from the past: Jeremy Taylor and Robert South from the seventeenth century and Archbishop Thomas Secker from the middle of the eighteenth. Here was a spirituality that was rational, moderate and centrally concerned with moral obligation. This High Church tradition, however, was about to be transformed.

The agent of the revolution was the Oxford Movement. The Tractarians, so-called because of the series of *Tracts for the Times* that they issued from Oxford from 1833 to 1841, urged the Church of England to claim a Catholic heritage. Their body, they contended, was the Anglo-Catholic Church. They downplayed its Protestant character, arguing for the continuity of the national church through the convulsions of the Reformation. That assertion more than any other brought down on them the wrath of a nation whose very identity was bound up with Protestantism. It needed strong-minded leaders to be so bold. These were John Henry Newman, possessing an acute mind and a prolific pen, a master of English prose who was to secede to Rome in 1845 and eventually become a cardinal; John Keble, essentially a parish clergyman at Hursley in Hampshire but who held the non-resident chair of poetry at Oxford; and Edward Bouverie Pusey, Professor of Hebrew

---

[2] Charlotte M. Yonge, *Chantry House*, London, 1889 edn, p. 14.

and an immensely learned man, especially in patristics. All were of a devout cast of mind. The discourse that stood first in Newman's earliest collection of sermons, published in 1835, was called 'Holiness Necessary for Future Blessedness':

> be quite sure [he declared] that a man who is contented with his own proficiency in Christian holiness, is at best in a dark state, or rather in great peril. If we are really imbued with the grace of holiness, we shall abhor sin as something base, irrational, and polluting.[3]

Keble composed the devotional handbook of the movement, *The Christian Year* (1827). Its verse, designed to illustrate the annual cycle of *The Book of Common Prayer*, nurtured the piety of thousands in subsequent generations. And Pusey was known to be rigorous in his own religious discipline, becoming pastoral mentor to hundreds of undergraduates at Oxford during his long life down to 1879. His correspondence contains a wealth of unhurried advice about the nourishing of the Christian life. The trio were devoted to the practice and propagation of a spirituality that they were not afraid to call Catholic.

What was the attitude of the Oxford Movement towards Evangelicalism? The Tractarians did not regard Evangelicals as the grand enemy because that role was reserved for the Latitudinarians, the representatives of the dominant liberal temper in the Georgian church. They were perceived as rationalistic in doctrine and lax in practice. The eighteenth century, according to the Oxford men, was a time when love had grown cold. The leaders of the Oxford Movement hoped to recruit Evangelicals to their cause of rekindling devotional warmth. Recent secondary literature, especially David Newsome's *The Parting of Friends*, has therefore tended to stress the continuity of Tractarianism with Evangelicalism.[4] There is much cogency in this case: Newman in particular

---

[3] J. H. Newman, *Parochial Sermons*, vol. 1, 2nd edn, London, 1835, p. 15.
[4] D. Newsome, *The Parting of Friends*, London, 1966.

began as an Evangelical, possessed Evangelical preoccupations such as the second advent in the 1830s and, as Sheridan Gilley's biography shows, retained much that was Evangelical throughout his life.[5]

Yet there is another side to this question, for many of the writings of the Tractarians were consciously designed to engage in debate with Evangelicalism. Their constant aim was to reveal its inadequacy. Thus Frederick Oakeley, who carried Oxford influences to London, announced unambiguously in 1839 that this 'modern system of theology' favoured 'self-indulgence and unscrupulousness'.[6] Newman, with a touch of the paradox he loved, described Evangelicalism as 'utterly unevangelical'.[7] The Oxford Movement had different theological concerns. For Evangelicals, as will appear, the central doctrine was the atonement: it was in dying on the cross that Christ redeemed humanity. For Tractarians, however, the central doctrine was the incarnation, the taking of flesh by the Son of God. They did not repudiate the atonement. They accepted the Evangelical view as more or less valid, but claimed that the cross had to be placed in a wider context. By his incarnation, they insisted, Christ identified with humanity in order to enable human beings to identify with God. The position is most fully stated in *The Doctrine of the Incarnation* (1848) by Robert Wilberforce, the son of the emancipator, who became a leading Anglo-Catholic theologian and then, in 1854, a Roman Catholic. Christ, according to Wilberforce, was the 'pattern man' to whom each human being must approximate through sacramental grace.[8] The incarnation supplanted the atonement as the fulcrum of theology. Boyd Hilton has argued in *The Age of Atonement* that the

[5] S. Gilley, *Newman and his Age*, London, 1990.

[6] F. Oakeley, *Sermons preached chiefly in the Chapel Royal at Whitehall*, Oxford, 1839, p. xix.

[7] J. H. Newman, *Parochial Sermons*, vol. 2, 2nd edn, London, 1836, p. 191.

[8] R. I. Wilberforce, *The Doctrine of the Incarnation of Our Lord Jesus Christ in its Relation to Mankind and to the Church*, London, 1848, chaps 1–4.

Evangelical movement shaped the language of social theory in all spheres in the earlier nineteenth century.[9] Metaphors relating to the atonement permeated economics and politics. From the 1860s, however, the cross ceased to provide the dominant motifs, being succeeded by themes relating to the incarnation. The change was partly because of the emergence of Broad Churchmen who dwelt on a humanitarian Christ; but equally it was because of the rise of a High Church party taking its cue from the Oxford Movement. Anglo-Catholics had a different focus for their piety from Evangelicals.

Hilton's persuasive overall case illustrates that religion had a profound influence upon nineteenth-century culture. In the present studies, however, one purpose is to show that religion, and ideas of holiness in particular, were shaped to a large extent by the culture of nineteenth-century England. Religion not only affects its host culture; it is also moulded by its cultural setting. The word 'culture' in this context calls for some comment. The term has been used in several ways. It often denotes 'high' culture, that is the expressions of civilisation in works of art, whether music, literature or the visual arts. In the nineteenth century the phrase might refer to the verse of Tennyson or the painting of Burne-Jones. Yet it may also mean something rather different. It may be applied to 'popular' culture, the manifestations of traditional folkways or of commercialised mass production. Thus it might mean customs such as dancing round the maypole or soap operas such as *Coronation Street*. And, again, it may signify something altogether more wide-embracing. Culture in the broadest sense may be defined as the web of attitudes and behaviour in a particular group. That is the standard usage in anthropology and, in consequence, missiology. Because this application is so wide, it takes in the other two meanings of the term. That is the way in which the word is used here. It includes the forms of high art that gradually shaped popular types of social expression; but it means the whole range of preconceptions that tinctured the ways in which people

---

[9]   B. Hilton, *The Age of Atonement: The Influence of Evangelicalism on Social and Economic Thought, 1785–1865*, Oxford, 1988.

thought and behaved. How did culture in this sense impinge on High Church spirituality?

The answer is primarily through Romanticism. The new mood usually called Romanticism began amongst the littérateurs, especially in Germany, in the later eighteenth century. In Britain it was represented most adequately, on its poetic side, by the Lake Poets, William Wordsworth and Samuel Taylor Coleridge, and, in prose, by the novelist Sir Walter Scott. The term, however, is not being confined here to the generation at the opening of the nineteenth century. Rather, it is being applied to the cultural wave that spread out from them, enveloping first some of the highly educated, and then slowly submerging an increasing proportion of the population. It was a long-term process: it lasted the whole of the century and beyond, well into the twentieth century. Romanticism was a reaction against the preceding Enlightenment, which will be considered in the next chapter. Whereas the Enlightenment had stressed reason and calculation, Romanticism emphasised will and emotion. For all its diversity, it normally exalted intuition, dwelt on mystery and advocated the natural against the artificial, the ancient against the modern. Its initial impact on the churches was felt in the second quarter of the nineteenth century, as Romantic taste began to diffuse from the literary avant-garde to a wider public. The Oxford Movement, as has often been suggested, should be seen as an embodiment of the Romantic temper in religion.[10] Newman said as much himself:

> What is Christian high-mindedness, generous self-denial, contempt of wealth, endurance of suffering, and earnest striving after perfection, but an improvement and transformation, under the influence of the Holy Spirit, of that natural character of mind which we call romantic?[11]

---

[10] Y. Brilioth, *The Anglican Revival: Studies in the Oxford Movement*, London, 1925, pp. 56–76; S. Prickett, *Romanticism and Religion*, Cambridge, 1976; M. Bright, 'English Literary Romanticism and the Oxford Movement', *Journal of the History of Ideas*, 40, 1979, pp. 385–404.

[11] Newman, *Parochial Sermons*, vol. 2, p. 59.

Thus the Anglo-Catholic quest for holiness – the 'earnest striving after perfection' – was coloured by the spirit of Romanticism. That emerges from an analysis, to which we now turn, of the spiritual tradition stemming from the Oxford Movement.

The Romantic tone is evident, first of all, in the Tractarian attitude to faith. In Enlightenment thought, reason typically receives knowledge from sense experience, being entirely passive in the process. By contrast, according to Romantics in general, the highest knowledge comes not through the understanding at all, but through intuition, or perhaps the imagination, which takes an active part in its acquisition. Faith, for Tractarians, is a similarly visionary faculty. For Newman, it is something apart from reason, though related to it, a different human power, morally conditioned. Henry Manning, one of the ablest disciples of the Oxford Movement, who, like Newman, was to end his days as a Roman Catholic cardinal, spoke of faith as a species of imagination, 'a spiritual consciousness of the world unseen'.[12] For Pusey, it was a faculty given 'instead of eyes'.[13] Because they held that faith gave a capacity of perception superior to reason, adherents of the Oxford Movement rejected the eighteenth-century style of apologetic based on the evidences of the Christian religion. There was no need to construct elaborate structures of argumentation in order to bring home a conviction of the validity of Christianity. Indeed it seemed profane to attempt to reason one's way to the Almighty when the correct attitude was to accept his gracious disclosure to the eye of faith. Therefore the early Tractarians abandoned the received method of natural theology that contended for the existence of God on the evidence of his works in creation. They saw religion as being entirely distinct from the natural science that the eighteenth century had pursued so eagerly. The sciences which experiment on material things, according to Newman, tend to make us 'forget the existence of Spirit and the Lord of

---

[12] H. E. Manning, 'The Intuition of Faith', *Sermons*, vol. 4, London, 1850, p. 377.

[13] E. B. Pusey, 'Faith', *Parochial Sermons*, vol. 2, Oxford, 1853, p. 1.

Spirits'.[14] Faith was the avenue to whatever knowledge was worth knowing. That attitude was symptomatic of the Romantic temper of the movement.

The typical Romantic had a large place for symbol. Coleridge in particular, in verse and prose, dwelt on symbols – the albatross, for example, in *The Ancient Mariner*. Coleridge, according to Newman, instilled 'a higher philosophy' into the enquiring minds of his own generation,[15] and so it is no surprise that symbolism pervaded the Oxford Movement. It led Tractarians to feel it natural to put the sacraments at the heart of the devotional life. 'Christ shines through the sacraments', declared Newman, 'as through transparent bodies, without impediment.'[16] The sacramental system was more powerful than preaching as a source of spiritual sustenance. Baptism was in fact the taproot of all grace. High Churchmen of all stripes believed in baptismal regeneration. Baptism, whether of an adult or of an infant, is the planting of Christian seed in the soul. Three of the most substantial *Tracts for the Times*, all by Pusey, were written to vindicate baptismal regeneration. In the waters of the font lay the divine power to wash away sin. There could be no clearer testimony to the potency of symbols to the Oxford Movement.

The eucharist was likewise given much greater weight than in the eighteenth century, which had looked at the communion service in very rational terms. At that time, there were two prevailing theories of the eucharist. According to receptionism, Christ's body and blood were not in the elements themselves; but the worthy recipient did receive the body and blood to sustain spiritual life. According to virtualism, the other theory, Christ's body and blood were not absolutely in the elements; but they were virtually so, in spirit, power and effect.[17] Even Walter Hook, the vicar of Leeds and

---

[14] Newman, *Parochial Sermons*, vol. 1, p. 260.
[15] J. H. Newman, *Apologia pro Vita Sua*, ed. M. Svaglic, Oxford, 1967, p. 94.
[16] Newman, *Parochial Sermons*, vol. 3, London, 1836, p. 302.
[17] A. Härdelin, *The Tractarian Understanding of the Eucharist*, Uppsala, 1965, pp. 125–6.

one of the leaders of the old High Church party, accepted virtualism.[18] But this position did not satisfy the Tractarians. They came to teach that Christ's body and blood were fully in the elements. In 1843 Pusey created a great stir by asserting in a university sermon the real presence of Christ in the bread and wine. Oxford was outraged at what seemed popish doctrine, and the vice-chancellor prohibited Pusey from preaching for two years. But Pusey believed that since Christ himself had said, 'This is my body' and 'This is my blood', his words were to be reverently accepted at their face value. It was easier for minds attuned to symbolism to see how something material could also be something spiritual. The Tractarians taught that the eucharist is the chief way in which believers become united with Christ, for it is the means by which his incarnate body is given to us. Eucharist and incarnation belonged together, so that the rite was rooted in the heart of their theology. In consequence they contended that the communion service must be held much more frequently than the previous norm of four times a year. Newman introduced weekly communion at his church of St Mary the Virgin in Oxford from 1837.[19] As Anglo-Catholic influence spread during the second half of the century, so did the practice of holding a weekly communion. In London in 1858, only 6 per cent of parish churches celebrated a eucharist every week; in 1882, fully 54 per cent did so.[20] Robert Wilberforce even encouraged a daily reception, a custom which became common among the more advanced disciples of the Oxford Movement later in the century.[21] In practice as in theory, there was an exalting of the place of the eucharist in the devotional life.

Worship in general was similarly upgraded. It was to be more of a priority than among many Evangelicals; and it was

---

[18] W. F. Hook, *The Eucharist a Sacrament and a Sacrifice*, London, 1847, pp. 10–11.
[19] Härdelin, *Tractarian Understanding*, p. 274.
[20] N. Temperley, *The Music of the English Parish Church*, Cambridge, 1979, vol. 1, p. 279.
[21] R. I. Wilberforce, *The Doctrine of the Holy Eucharist*, 2nd edn, London, 1853, p. 370.

to be more charged with awe than among previous generations of High Churchmen. Church was the place to revere the mystery of God, in whom, according to Pusey, 'greatness and indistinctness commence together'.[22] Previously parish churches had been public meeting places where the locals chatted with few inhibitions. Now, under the sway of the Tractarians, there was propagated the ideal of silence in church – or at most whispering. What took place in places of worship must be elaborate, dignified, appropriate to a sacred place. There was a flowering of liturgical developments. While it is true that the early leaders of the Oxford Movement did not stress ritual, even in the later 1830s there were the tentative beginnings of higher practices. Already officiants at Holy Communion were wearing scarves with embroidered crosses and lighted candlesticks were being placed on the communion table. The taste for greater ceremonial spread, giving rise to the advancing tide of ritualism that marked the second half of the century in the Church of England. Wafer bread was adopted for the eucharist, water was mixed with wine in the chalice, and even incense was employed by the most advanced brethren before the century was out. The most popular innovation was the wearing by the preacher in the pulpit of a white surplice instead of the traditional black gown. The surplice represented the teaching authority of the church; the desuetude of the gown marked a break with the Protestant past. By 1882 nearly three-quarters of the parish churches of London had taken up the practice.[23] Only stick-in-the-mud clergy and diehard Evangelicals, who were sometimes the same individuals, resisted what they saw as unwarranted clericalism. Ritualism carried symbolism into every part of public worship.

The setting of worship was also treated as having sacred significance. The building, Newman believed, could speak of Christ.[24] The crucial development in this area took place not at

---

[22] Quoted from Pusey's lectures on 'Types and Prophecies' by G. Rowell, *The Vision Glorious: Themes and Personalities of the Catholic Revival in Anglicanism*, Oxford, 1983, p. 77.

[23] Temperley, *Music of the English Parish Church*, vol. 1, p. 279.

Oxford, but at Cambridge. There, in 1839, was founded the Cambridge Camden Society for the study of ecclesiastical architecture. The new society set about what it called ecclesiology, the systematic examination of mediaeval church buildings to discover the message conveyed by each of their parts. Its members considered, for example, that the tilting of the chancel slightly south of the line of the nave might have represented the head of the dying Christ on the cross, lolling unsupported to one side. However fanciful the society's interpretations, the fashion for Gothic architecture for new buildings that it promoted, already gathering momentum, soon became well-nigh universal. Perhaps the greatest monument to the Tractarian ideal was William Butterfield's All Saints, Margaret Street, in London. Every inch of the interior was blanketed with colour, a riot of fresco, brickwork, encaustic tiles and stained glass. The beauty of the building, it was thought, could be enhanced by decorations. It was only in the Victorian period that there grew up the custom of putting fresh flowers in church. At first this practice was sternly denounced by Evangelicals as another ritualist corruption. And beauty could be heard as well as seen. Although it has been established that chanting and other musical innovations in the parish churches of the nineteenth century were first introduced before the rise of the Oxford Movement, there is no doubt that the movement was associated with their spread. The traditional village musicians in the rear gallery, vividly portrayed in Thomas Hardy's *Under the Greenwood Tree*, were banished. They were replaced by surpliced choirs of men and boys. By 1882 more than half the London parish churches enjoyed the resulting cathedral style of worship.[25] These changes were all designed to enhance the impact of worship in aesthetic, non-rational, often subliminal ways. They were a tribute to the appeal of symbol in a Romantic age.

The Tractarians and their followers also showed a penchant for poetry in the manner of the Romantics. Keble dedicated

---

[24] Newman, *Parochial Sermons*, vol. 6, London, 1842, p. 331.

[25] Temperley, *Music of the English Parish Church*, vol. 1, p. 279.

the published version of his lectures as Professor of Poetry to Wordsworth, calling him a 'True Philosopher and Inspired Poet'.[26] Keble's *Christian Year*, the author explained, was designed to express his feelings in a disciplined way, very much echoing Wordsworth's aesthetic. Charlotte M. Yonge, a resident in Keble's parish, wrote fiction in order to propagate his ideals, even submitting some of the novels to him for his censorship. In *Chantry House* she describes the holiday trip of a family that had fallen under the spell of the Oxford Movement. First they read together from *The Christian Year*:

> And then a turning to the 'Ode to Immortality', for Wordsworth was our second leader, and we carried him on our tour as our one secular book, as Keble was our one religious book.[27]

In view of the ascendancy of Wordsworth, it is not surprising that Tractarian piety embraced a reverence for nature. Newman dismissed any understanding of the natural world as 'mere mechanical processes'.[28] Keble wrote in his verse of natural forces as a semi-sacramental expression of the divine in such frequently recurring words as 'dew', 'light' and 'radiance'. Seeing the natural world as charged with the supernatural has been seen as the essence of Romanticism.[29]

The rise of Romantic sensibility was closely bound up with a new feeling for history in the early nineteenth century. The Enlightenment had tended to dismiss whatever was old as likely to be corrupt and useless, and certainly in need of modernisation. The Romantics, by contrast, normally thought of the old as conveying an ancient wisdom. The venerable was to be respected; the past had value in itself. Sir Walter Scott's novels recreated the world of the past, vividly evoking, in *Ivanhoe*, the pageantry of the middle ages. Scott,

---

[26] J. Keble, *Lectures on Poetry*, trans. E. K. Francis, Oxford, 1912, vol. 1, p. 8.
[27] Yonge, *Chantry House*, p. 226.
[28] Newman, *Parochial Sermons*, vol. 2, p. 406.
[29] M. H. Abrams, *Natural Supernaturalism: Tradition and Revolution in Romantic Literature*, London, 1971.

according to Newman, prepared the way for the Oxford Movement by turning minds 'to the direction of the middle ages'.[30] Scott's Gothic vision is evident in the poem 'The Baptistery' by Isaac Williams, another prominent Tractarian. The poem is set in the moonlit ruins of St David's Cathedral:

> I slowly wander'd through the site
> Of crumbling walls, half-falling tower,
> Mullions and arch, which darkly lower
> And o'er the intruder seem to frown,
> Putting on size beyond their own,
> Like giants in enchanted tale,
> As dimly seen through misty veil.[31]

The same enthusiasm for the mediaeval struck deepest root in Hurrell Froude, like Newman, a fellow of Oriel College, Oxford. For Froude the Reformation, the destroyer of the age of faith, was a bugbear. When, in 1838, Newman published his writings posthumously, they provoked Protestant outrage. But others went even further, celebrating the saints of the middle ages in hagiographical style. F. W. Faber, who was shortly to transfer his allegiance to Rome, issued in 1844 a *Life of Saint Wilfrid*, the champion of Roman against Celtic claims at the Synod of Whitby of 664. And soon John Mason Neale translated an abundance of mediaeval hymns from Latin into English. Many appeared in *Hymns Ancient and Modern* (1860), originally a partisan manifesto of Anglo-Catholic devotion. All this was part and parcel of the Romantic mediaevalism that marked the century.

The historic sense, however, pushed the Tractarians further back, to the early Fathers of the church. Keble wanted to turn to 'the apostolical age' for guidance;[32] Newman wrote on the Arian controversy; and Pusey's patristic scholarship was massive. The ancient texts were used in the first instance to

---

[30] Newman, *Apologia*, p. 94.
[31] I. Williams, 'The Baptistery', p. 194, quoted by O. Chadwick, *The Mind of the Oxford Movement*, London, 1960, p. 69.
[32] Quoted by Chadwick, *Mind of the Oxford Movement*, p. 39.

interpret the Bible. The method can be illustrated by Pusey's treatment of John 3:5: 'Except a man be born of water and of the Spirit he cannot enter the kingdom of God.' Many commentators denied that 'water' referred to baptism, but Pusey appealed to the Fathers and the ancient liturgies to show that they took the verse in that sense. Hence, the theologian concluded, this text implies baptismal regeneration.[33] The technique deployed patristic sources as a tool for the understanding of Scripture, to which they were subordinate. Yet the elevation of the Fathers did detract from the unique status of the Bible. Newman could write as early as 1836 that the true test of religious teaching was the rule of 'Scripture and Antiquity'.[34] The equal yoking implies a higher place for ancient tradition than had normally been accepted, even by High Churchmen, in the past. It contrasted sharply, as will appear in subsequent chapters, with the simple biblicism of the Evangelicals.

The appeal to the ancient church gave the Tractarians a fellow-feeling with certain seventeenth-century churchmen, especially the so-called Caroline divines, Bishop Lancelot Andrewes and Archbishop William Laud. The prayers of these men enjoyed a fresh vogue.

> Bishop Andrews' Devotions [observed Pusey] so entirely express the wants and desires of a mind trained in the teaching of the ancient Church, that one feels the more confident as to the sameness of his doctrine.[35]

---

[33] E. B. Pusey, *Scriptural Views of Holy Baptism, as Established by the Consent of the Ancient Church, and Contrasted with the Systems of Modern Schools, Tracts for the Times*, No. 67, 3rd edn, Oxford, 1835, pp. 30–1.
[34] Newman, *Parochial Sermons*, vol. 2, p. iv.
[35] E. B. Pusey, *Preface to the Fourth Edition of the 'Letter to the Right Reverend Father in God, Richard, Lord Bishop of Oxford, on the Tendency to Romanism imputed to Doctrines held of Old, as Now, in the English Church': On the Doctrine of Justification*, Oxford, 1840, note on p. xlii.

Andrewes and Laud were truly Catholic in spirit. The Tractarians recruited them into a particular tradition within Anglicanism with which they could identify. From the late seventeenth century they added Bishop Jeremy Taylor, and from the eighteenth Bishop Thomas Wilson. These seemed to be men who had upheld the principles of High Church devotion amidst the arid wastes of neglect. The Oxford Movement was engaging in a typical venture of the nineteenth century inspired by the Romantic love for the past, the invention of tradition. The figures the Tractarians chose had not previously been linked in a chain that excluded other Anglican divines. The past was raided selectively in order to legitimate preferences in the present. But consequently the writings of these authors proved particularly influential in moulding subsequent High Church spirituality.

From this combination of sources, mediaeval, ancient and Caroline, the Oxford Movement gained a fresh sense of the value of asceticism. Actions of self-denial, according to Isaac Williams, 'dispose the heart to prayer'.[36] No-one took the principle further than Pusey. After the death of his wife in 1839, he became obsessive about the need to deny himself any self-indulgence. In old age he was described as having a 'perfectly pallid, furrowed, mortified face'.[37] Matters had been pushed to an extreme with his family. When his son failed to make adequate religious progress, Pusey birched him. If his son did show progress, the bundle of birches was reduced by one twig.[38] The Tractarians in general advocated fasting: Pusey's first tract, number 18, was on the subject. Abstinence was especially to be practised in Lent in preparation for Passiontide. Some adopted a rule of life that included fasting, almsgiving and other pious deeds. This craving for spiritual discipline led to the revival of monastic communities in the Church of England. The first woman was professed into the

---

[36] I. Williams, *Tracts for the Times*, No. 80, p. 41.

[37] H. P. Liddon, *Life of Edward Bouverie Pusey*, 4th edn, London, 1898, vol. 3, p. 60.

[38] H. C. G. Matthew, 'Edward Bouverie Pusey: From Scholar to Tractarian', *Journal of Theological Studies*, 32, 1981, p. 116.

religious life as early as 1841, though at that time there was no community for her to join. Between 1845 and 1900 fully sixty-two Anglican religious orders were founded for women; in the same period fifteen were established for men.[39] Many sacrificed glittering prospects, and all gave up comfort, for the sake of observing a rigorous holy life. It was one of the consequences of looking to the past for ideals of sanctity to pursue in the present.

A further Romantic theme that outcrops in Tractarian practice was growth. If a central metaphor of the Enlightenment for understanding human society was the machine, for nineteenth-century Romanticism an equivalent was the tree. The model was part of nature; and it was dynamic rather than static. Human beings, it was felt, went through an organic process of growing to maturity that paralleled the development of, say, an acorn into an oak. The Christian life was therefore conceived as a burgeoning of the spirituality within. Although, as we shall see, there was an important place for dramatic change in the Romantic psyche, it dwelt above all on process. Habit was the great principle of growth. 'Every act of obedience,' according to Newman, 'has a tendency to strengthen our conviction about heaven. Every sacrifice makes us more zealous; every self-denial makes us more devoted.'[40] So character ripened slowly for heaven – or its opposite. Charlotte M. Yonge's *Chantry House* is the story of two brothers within the parameters of Tractarian piety. One, Clarence, steadily adopts good habits; the older brother, Griff, marries foolishly and lapses into bad ways. 'It has been all up, up with him,' muses the dying Griff about Clarence, 'all down, down with me.'[41] The teaching about the steady evolution of the disposition created a contrast with standard Evangelical opinion. Evangelicals stressed the need for conversion, often a crisis, as the opening of the Christian life. The Oxford

[39] P. F. Anson, *The Call of the Cloister: Religious Communities and Kindred Bodies in the Anglican Communion*, London, 1958, pp. 591–4.

[40] Newman, *Parochial Sermons*, vol. 6, p. 109.

[41] Yonge, *Chantry House*, p. 330.

Movement did not altogether deny the importance of this kind of conversion. Pusey accepted that there was a first turning to God which could properly be called conversion. Yet all Tractarians believed that the seed of faith was planted in the soul at baptism. Hence conversion could never have the ultimate significance it possessed for Evangelicals of determining the destination of heaven or hell for the individual. Pusey preferred to speak of conversion as 'a course of being conformed to God' that lasted the whole lifetime.[42] Religious progress was evolutionary rather than revolutionary.

The Romantic temper had a further characteristic. Whereas the Enlightenment had attached importance to the particular, the unit, Romanticism normally looked to the whole, the corporate. That is not to deny the preoccupation of many Romantics with individuality, the fruit of the personal growth that has just been considered; but it is to draw attention to their typical disavowal of individualism for the sake of bringing out the solidarity of the group. Romanticism was famously the intellectual seedbed of the awareness of nationhood that sprang up all over Europe during the nineteenth century. The nation was often equated with the corporate identity of the speakers of a single tongue. In a similar way the Oxford Movement saw the church as the corporate identity of the professors of a single faith. The church reflected, in fact, the genius of the people who upheld it, so that Tractarians often spoke with affection of 'the English Church'. It was through participation in her life and worship that anyone might hope for salvation. Religion was very much a community affair. The church had unity, however, not because it was a human organisation, the established Church of England, but because it was a divine creation, a legitimate section of the Catholic Church. Hence individuals should renounce their private judgement in order to defer to ecclesiastical authority. Here again was a great contrast with the Evangelical position at the time, which gloried in the right of private judgement in the interpretation of Scripture. For the Tractarian, virtue lay in accepting the judgement of the

---

[42] E. B. Pusey, *Parochial Sermons* vol. 3, Oxford, 1873, p. 20.

divinely guided Christian community. Spiritual health lay in submission to the church.

One corollary was an exalted role for the clergyman as the commissioned representative of the Holy Catholic Church. Newman urged the clerical readers of the very first *Tract for the Times* to 'magnify your office'.[43] How great, he declared in a later sermon, 'must be the sin of resisting the ministers of Christ'.[44] The whole Oxford Movement was decidedly clericalist. There were consequences for ritual. At the eucharist, it was believed, the minister acted as a true priest, offering in some sense the sacrifice of the body and blood of Christ. Hence any clergyman influenced by the movement adopted not the traditional north end position at the communion table but the eastward position. He faced east, with his back to the congregation, to show that he was representing them before God. This was the liturgical innovation the Evangelicals resisted most steadfastly throughout the nineteenth century and, in many cases, long into the twentieth. They could not accept the Anglo-Catholic premise that the minister occupied a representative priestly office. They were also repelled by another development in the clerical role. From 1846 Pusey publicly advocated auricular confession. Any Christian, he held, should seek to confess his sins to a priest so that he could receive confidential guidance and sacramental absolution. Orthodox High Churchmen of the traditional type had never accepted this practice, treating it as one of the corruptions of Rome. But it was a reasonable deduction from revering the divine commission of the clergy. They were the officers of a church with high prerogatives.

If the corporate loomed so large in the Tractarian worldview, the place of individual experience was correspondingly lowered. It was the common life of the church that mattered, not the vagaries of personal religiosity. The Oxford Movement tended to share the Orthodox High Church wariness of emotion: 'men,' wrote Newman, 'may have their religious feelings roused, without being on that

---

[43] J. H. Newman, *Tracts for the Times*, No. 1, p. 4.
[44] Newman, *Parochial Sermons*, vol. 4, p. 320.

account *at all* the more likely to obey God in practice.'[45] Newman and Pusey both deprecated what they called 'religious excitements'. True religion, according to the Oxford men, was calm, even-tempered, an embodiment of peace. This is where the Tractarian doctrine of reserve fitted in. The tracts commended the view that some things were too holy, too personal, to be fit subjects for conversation. In particular, experience of the power of the atonement was not to be cast as pearls before swine. The cross of Christ, declared Newman, was the heart of religion, but in a human being the heart was hidden from view: 'and so in like manner the sacred doctrine of the Atoning Sacrifice is not to be talked of, but to be lived upon; not to be put forth boldly, but to be adored privately'.[46] Newman and his friends decried bearing testimony to what God had done for the soul. There is only one place to profess openly, he said tartly, and that is in church.[47] The anti-Evangelical drift of these remarks will be apparent.

The culmination of this tendency was in the attitude of the Oxford Movement and its followers to the Evangelical view of assurance. It was common ground among Evangelicals, Calvinist as well as Arminian, that assurance of salvation was to be expected. The Christian could know that his sins were forgiven, that he was right with God. Tractarians were unhappy with this conviction on two scores. For one thing, it rested, they believed, on taking faith to be a feeling, a matter of sense experience. That was to rely on subjective human affections rather than on objective divine grace mediated through the sacraments. In the second place, they held that it created a false sense of security. They rejected the Calvinist teaching that true believers cannot fall away from faith and so in the end be numbered among the lost. There could be no certainty of salvation. A person, contended Newman, may claim assurance of faith.

---

[45] Ibid., vol. 1, p. 205.
[46] Ibid., vol. 6, pp. 98–9.
[47] Ibid., vol. 1, p. 202.

True; but where does Scripture tell us that such an assurance, without grounds for it beyond our feeling it, comes from God? where is it promised? till it is found then, we must be content not to be sure, and to fear and hope about ourselves at once.[48]

So there was a fundamental difference between Evangelical and High Church piety. The Evangelical was sure he was on the road to heaven and so urged others to join him; the Anglo-Catholic doubted whether he would reach the destination and so used all the traveller's aids provided by the church to help him on his journey.

Tractarian spirituality, then, was associated with symbol, history, growth and the corporate. It was a remodelling of the High Church tradition by the new Romantic taste of the nineteenth century. That cultural preference, however, was not distributed equally at all levels in society. Workers in the mills or the mines rarely had time or inclination to delve into such novelties. Preoccupations of any kind, whether poetry or religion, that were Romantic in flavour were far more the province of the elite. Those who had time and leisure to read the latest ideas were the most likely to be swayed by the new cultural mood. High Churchmanship was therefore very much an elite affair in the nineteenth century. Admittedly it is true that in the later Victorian years slum priests carried ritualism into urban parishes, drawing in some of the working people. But those were exceptions, celebrated because they were indeed exceptional. Priests inspired by Tractarian ideals tended to serve prosperous suburban parishes; and the clergy were overwhelmingly upper-class or upper middle-class in background. At the end of the century over two-thirds of the Anglo-Catholic clergy were Oxford or Cambridge graduates.[49] The Tractarian ethos attracted young aristocrats. The son of Lord Shaftesbury, the great Evangelical philanthropist, for example, adopted High Church views, erecting a vast and gaudy rood screen in the parish church hard by his Dorset

---

[48] Ibid., p. 145.
[49] W. S. F. Pickering, *Anglo-Catholicism: A Study in Religious Ambiguity*, London, 1989, p. 98.

home. High Church devotion was essentially an elite phenomenon in the nineteenth century.

It was in the twentieth century that a way of looking at the world tinctured by Romanticism spread to a wider public. The processes of cultural diffusion carried a Romantic sensibility to larger numbers and lower down the social scale. The remarkable range of books published in inter-war Britain called 'The Romance of . . .' bears testimony to the extent of the development. The change made spirituality in the Tractarian mode acceptable to a broader cross-section of the community. A series of Anglo-Catholic Congresses in the 1920s showed the increasing numbers and increasing confidence of the party. One of the Congress leaders, the missionary bishop Frank Weston of Zanzibar, has been described as 'a man who loved the dramatic gesture' and as 'medieval in his ascetic devotions'.[50] Clearly the Romantic manner generated by the Oxford Movement was still a growing force in inter-war England. It was in the post-war years that the prevailing tone of the Church of England became most Anglo-Catholic. The first Tractarian Archbishop of Canterbury, Michael Ramsey, was not consecrated until 1961. As Adrian Hastings has argued, the century saw a drift in nearly all churches in a Catholic direction.[51] So it was in the twentieth century rather than the nineteenth that the High Church tradition made its greatest mark on English popular piety. The triumph of the Oxford Movement came in the reign, not of Victoria, but of Elizabeth II.

---

[50] A. Hastings, *A History of English Christianity, 1920–1985*, London, 1986, p. 199.
[51] Ibid.

Chapter Two

The Calvinist Tradition

A second, and very different, version of holiness was the one arising from Calvinism. The Calvinist, or Reformed, tradition stemmed from John Calvin, the sixteenth-century reformer of Geneva. Whereas in Scotland it dominated the religious landscape through Presbyterianism, in England it appeared in two guises, in the established church and in Dissent. It had flourished among the Puritans within the Church of England during the seventeenth century. Although the Reformed tradition faded away as the broader theology of the Latitudinarians advanced, the Evangelical Revival of the eighteenth century brought it back to life in the established church. Not all the Anglican Evangelicals were Calvinists, and Charles Simeon, the greatest of their number around 1800, soon afterwards repudiated the label. But most of them embraced a form of Calvinism, so that the Reformed position was their starting point at the beginning of the nineteenth century. In Dissent, by contrast, there was continuity in the Reformed tradition between the Puritan teaching of the seventeenth century and the theological position of their nineteenth-century descendants in the faith. Originally three denominations, the Presbyterians, the Independents (or Congregationalists) and the Baptists, were Calvinistic. During the eighteenth century, however, the Presbyterians were strongly affected by rationalism, so that most of them gradually abandoned a Calvinist faith in favour of Unitarianism. The Congregationalists and the Baptists, on the other hand, generally maintained their orthodoxy and their Calvinism. The groups that drew their theology from Calvinist sources in the nineteenth century

were therefore the Evangelical Anglicans, the Congregationalists and the Baptists.

The Reformed tradition altered greatly over time. The
content of Calvinist teaching has sometimes been supposed,
by friends as well as foes, to have remained substantially
unchanged down the centuries. Yet in reality received opinion
in the nineteenth century was very different from what had
prevailed two hundred years before. There has been increasing
appreciation by historians that Reformed doctrine varied
from age to age: the place given to predestination, in
particular, rose and fell between Calvin himself and the
Victorian era. But it is less recognised that there were also
transformations in spirituality. The Puritan piety of the
seventeenth century followed a distinctive pattern. The predestination of the elect to salvation was the starting point. Not
everybody had an opportunity of reaching heaven. The
supreme question for each individual was therefore: am I one
of the elect? Even in devoted Christians there was the fear that
their faith would prove to be counterfeit and they would turn
out to be castaways. Puritan pastors deliberately encouraged
their flocks to doubt the authenticity of their discipleship so
that they would commit all their energies to the spiritual quest.
Ministers frequently urged the members of their congregations to 'make their calling and election sure', that is, to search
for marks of election in their lives. Only if they passed through
intense exercises of soul would they stick close to Christ. The
tone of spirituality was therefore halting and anxious. Many
Puritans would shrink from approaching the Lord's Table.
Although the Westminster Confession stated that assurance of
being in a state of grace is attainable, nevertheless 'a true
believer may wait long, and conflict with many difficulties
before he be a partaker of it'.[1] This was the condition described
by Max Weber in his classic thesis about Protestantism giving
rise to capitalism.[2] Weber referred not to Protestants in
general, nor even to Calvinists in general, but specifically to

---

[1] *The Confession of Faith*, Edinburgh, 1810, chap. 18:3, p. 106.
[2] M. Weber, *The Protestant Ethic and the Spirit of Capitalism*,
London, 1930, chap. 4A.

the Calvinists of the seventeenth century. Their books of devotion, Weber noticed, directed them to examine themselves for signs of divine favour. Worldly success was one of the indications that sanctification had begun. Hence, in order to alleviate their fears, they strove with all their might and ingenuity for commercial achievement. The consequence was capitalism. We are not compelled to agree with Weber's hypothesis to appreciate his portrayal of seventeenth-century Reformed piety. Although there were notable exceptions such as John Bunyan, Calvinists of that epoch were encouraged to adopt an introspective and often rather gloomy style of devotion.

The Puritan style of spirituality did not disappear during the eighteenth century. Authors from the previous century were still read and the Dissenters who followed their counsel continued to agonise over their state. Change in the Reformed tradition was initially in the direction of a higher Calvinism. There was more, rather than less, emphasis on divine sovereignty. The greatest Baptist theologian of the mid-eighteenth century, John Gill, produced an elaborate scholastic system that accentuated the divine decrees. So there was little alleviation of personal anxieties as the core of the spiritual life.

Some divines, furthermore, went beyond Gill in exalting the part played by the Almighty in saving sinners. They asserted the doctrine of 'imputed sanctification'. When believers are accepted by Christ, on this view, they are not only accounted righteous in justification. They are also credited with holiness, without any work of the Holy Spirit to make their lives actually holy. Robert Hawker, the vicar of the parish of Charles in Plymouth from 1784 to 1827, was the main propagator of this teaching. He refused to preach the need for holiness of life, informing the Evangelical Anglican leader Charles Simeon that the only reason the apostles had done so was the then infant state of the church.[3] The Christian was as much sanctified at the start of his union with Christ as at its consummation. Ordinary Evangelicals such as Simeon

---

[3] G. Carter, 'Robert Hawker', in D. M. Lewis, ed., *The Blackwell Dictionary of Evangelical Biography*, Oxford, 1995, vol. 1, p. 537.

denounced this doctrine as undermining morality. It seemed tainted with antinomianism, the belief that the Christian is not under the moral law of God. Although Hawker denied the charge of antinomianism, other less circumspect figures gloried in their rejection of the moral law as the believer's rule of life. One such was William Huntington, a former coal-heaver and a high Calvinist preacher in London who added the initials 'S.S.' after his name to signify 'Sinner Saved'. Huntington was so high a Calvinist that he held that grace alone should be magnified, not law at all. The motive for doing right sprang from the gospel, not the divine commands. He was an outspoken controversialist.

> I believe [he declared] that none of those who have written against me, calling me antinomian, ever performed one good work in all their lives, being wholly destitute of a good root.[4]

Huntington was not a preacher of immorality, but others feared that his teaching veered that way. The tendency among certain Calvinists to teach a higher version of their faith led them to diminish, at least in theory, the sanctions of morality. The imperative to holiness seemed at risk.

That development, however, was not the prevailing trend at the opening of the nineteenth century. On the contrary, the chief trend was in precisely the opposite direction, towards a lower form of Calvinism. The major influence was the great eighteenth-century American theologian Jonathan Edwards, who, while remaining staunchly within the Reformed tradition, had modified it drastically. It is important to appreciate how Edwards's position differed from higher versions of the Calvinist faith because it was to become the template for much of the piety of the period down to 1900. The high Calvinists taught that only the Almighty, by irresistible grace, can bring about the conversion of sinners: the human contribution is

---

[4] W. Huntington, 'Every Divine Law in the Heart of Christ and his Spiritual Seed: But the Unbelieving Disobedient to the Faith and Without Law', *The Select Works of the Rev. William Huntington, S. S.*, London, 1856, vol. 3, p. 417.

non-existent, for human beings cannot turn to God by themselves. Edwards, however, drew a contrast between natural and moral inability. Natural inability operated when human beings could not do what they wanted to do. Moral inability operated when they did not do something because they did not want to do it. The latter, not the former, was true of those rejecting the gospel, who therefore bore culpability for their decision. Hence there was an obligation to believe the gospel, what came to be called duty faith. This view, unlike earlier Calvinism, was not fatalistic. In the previous understanding, the Almighty was responsible for the loss of the soul. This was the so-called doctrine of double predestination, according to which God chose some for heaven but condemned others to hell. The newer position was that the sinner was responsible for his own fate. This was the stance shared by Andrew Fuller among the Baptists and Edward Williams among the Independents. It became the prevailing version of the Reformed tradition in the nineteenth century, called 'strict Calvinism' by Fuller but often described as 'moderate Calvinism' by historians. It was this type of Calvinist teaching that fostered the spread of the gospel. If the Almighty had laid upon all human beings an obligation to believe, all must be allowed an opportunity to respond. Here was the theology that lay behind the first missionary societies of the 1790s – the Baptist Missionary Society, the Missionary Society (later the London Missionary Society, supported chiefly by Congregationalists) and the Church Missionary Society (C.M.S.). The Reformed tradition became as expansionist as Methodism in the early nineteenth century. It now upheld an Evangelical species of Calvinism.

Evangelical Calvinism was shaped by the Enlightenment. The high culture of the eighteenth century left an enduring legacy to the period that followed. The Enlightenment was an era that asserted the ability of human reason to discover truth. Descartes, John Locke and Sir Isaac Newton had prepared the way in the seventeenth century. All shared the view that inherited opinion should not be taken on trust. Rather, investigation was essential to establish true knowledge. The Enlightenment is often thought to have been intrinsically anti-religious, pitting human reason against divine revelation. Thus Voltaire wished to eliminate institutional religion, *écraser l'infâme*. But it has been increasingly recognised that the French Enlightenment was unusual in the degree of its virulence against religion. In northern Germany, the advocates of Enlightenment were closely bound up with Pietism. In southern Germany, Catholic reform appealed to Enlightenment values in arguing for the simplicity of the early Christians against scholastic intricacies and Jesuit intrigue.[5] In England, as B. W. Young has recently suggested, the position was similar.[6] The Latitudinarians of the Church of England wished to show the compatibility of reason and religion. Edmund Law, for instance, bishop of Carlisle from 1768 to 1787, was the editor of the works of Locke and a champion of toleration. The prevailing tone of the late eighteenth-century church was to incorporate Enlightenment insights into revealed religion.

Where the connection between Christianity and the Enlightenment is admitted, it is often assumed that the rise of reason in religion simply promoted unorthodoxy. It is true that the impact of the age of reason on the Presbyterians was in that direction. Their intellectual leadership was induced to reject the metaphysical abstractions of the past for the sake of following the teaching of the Bible alone. They therefore disowned any dogmas savouring of the mysterious, and especially the doctrine of the Trinity. They moved to Arianism and, under Joseph Priestley's influence in the later eighteenth century, many became Socinians, rejecting the deity of Christ. Hence 'rational Dissent' emerged as Unitarian in the nineteenth century because of the sway of the Enlightenment. That, however, was not the only way in which the cultural preoccupations of the period impinged on English religion.

---

[5] J. Whaley, 'The Protestant Enlightenment in Germany', and T. C. W. Blanning, 'The Enlightenment in Catholic Germany', in R. Porter and M. Teich, *The Enlightenment in National Context*, Cambridge, 1981.

[6] B. W. Young, *Religion and Enlightenment in Eighteenth-Century England*, Oxford, 1998.

The Evangelical movement itself shared the characteristics of the Enlightenment. The movement is often treated as an emotional reaction against the age of reason. Although there was a great deal of uninhibited excitement in and around the revival, such an estimate does not take account of the insistence of the Evangelical leaders that they were in no way downgrading reason. They revered Locke and Newton. They believed that in the intellectual methods of these men they had isolated the correct way of discovering truth. There must be toleration and free enquiry; empirical research must ascertain the facts. They believed in experiment: Evangelicalism was 'experimental religion'. What had been found by investigation could be known with confidence, whether in science or religion. Light had dawned in either case, for conversion was Christian enlightenment. Evangelicalism and the Enlightenment were closely aligned.

There were important consequences for the spiritual life. Evangelical Calvinists such as Andrew Fuller possessed a much stronger view of knowledge than their predecessors in the Reformed tradition. Calvinists of the seventeenth and eighteenth centuries, as we have seen, suffered from perennial doubt about their salvation. That was often still the case in the 1790s. Thus in that decade Elizabeth Bowden, the daughter of the Independent minister at Tooting, Surrey, fell seriously ill at the age of seventeen. Aware of the danger to her life, she was anxious and despondent. 'I want more comfort in my soul . . .' she told her father, 'I want to *know* my interest in the *covenant*.' Elizabeth evidently lacked assurance of her faith – though, since her last word as she died was 'Joys!', she seems to have found it in the end.[7] Others in the early nineteenth century likewise worried about whether they were of the elect and asked whether the promises of the gospel were for them. But as Fuller's teaching spread, so confidence in the knowledge of one's salvation became firmer. Richard Freeman, for instance, the son of a Baptist deacon at Plymouth, went to London, where in 1826, at the age of twenty-three, he suffered an

---

[7] *Evangelical Magazine*, March 1794, p. 121.

accident that confined him at home for nearly a year. A course
of self-examination led him to peace in believing. He received,
according to his obituarist, 'an assurance which it is believed
he never lost'. What he experienced was described as 'the witness of the Spirit', exactly the phrase used by Wesley for the
assurance of faith.[8] Freeman illustrates that by the earlier nineteenth century, the Calvinist tradition had come to approximate to Methodism. Both stressed the possibility of knowing
that one was saved. Hence the Christian life was no longer one
of constant anxiety. Doubt about one's spiritual status was
banished from the mind. The kernel of authentic piety was
now thought to be the confidence brought about by the certain
prospect of heaven.

For Calvinist Evangelicals – as for Methodists, as we shall
see – the holy life had four salient characteristics. For one
thing, it commenced with conversion.

> I believe [wrote a correspondent of *The Baptist Magazine* in
> 1809] all genuine Calvinists, as well as all pious Arminians,
> concur in regarding a radical change of the principles and
> dispositions of the mind, as essential to final salvation.[9]

A typical illustration is found in the life of Elizabeth, who later
married William Nichols, the pastor of North Collingham
Baptist Church, Nottinghamshire. There was a prelude.
Elizabeth's brother died of tuberculosis in 1808, when she was
twenty-two years old, and she 'discovered the depravity of her
heart'. She went to visit relations living ten miles away and
there meditated on the Bible and other devotional works.
Then came the turning point:

> one day walking alone in the fields . . . she was favoured with such
> a discovery of the love of God in the gift of his Son, and the love of
> Christ in dying for the redemption of sinners, as filled her soul
> with joy unspeakable, mingled with godly sorrow for her past
> sins, so that for some time she was unable to leave this highly

---

[8] *Baptist Magazine*, November 1850, p. 692.
[9] *Baptist Magazine*, February 1809, p. 50.

favoured spot, concerning which the words of Jacob might be adopted, *Surely God is in this place.*[10]

The time and place clearly made a vivid impression on Elizabeth, who was herself to die of tuberculosis only two years later. Although she did not dare speak of her enlightenment for some while, this crisis was the decisive event of her short life.

Not all Calvinists, however, underwent experiences so momentous. Another wife of a Baptist minister who died young was Mrs John Stock, born at Spalding, Lincolnshire, in 1822:

> so early and gradual was the work of grace upon her soul [reported her obituarist] that she could never refer to any particular period at which she was conscious of its commencement.[11]

Although this deficiency caused her some uneasiness, the obituarist, probably her husband, was in no doubt that there had indeed been a work of grace. For her, conversion had been both gradual and unconscious. The reality of this way of starting the Christian pilgrimage was acknowledged by virtually all of those who stood in the Reformed tradition. Robert Bickersteth, the strongly Evangelical bishop of Ripon from 1857 to 1884, 'did not insist', according to his son, 'on a sudden, sensible conversion'. Yet he taught that 'a conscious turning from sin to God was the crisis of the religious life, and the only true foundation of future peace and progress'.[12] Conversion dealt with the guilt of the past and set the believer on the path to greater resistance to future temptation. As the century wore on, it is true, there was often less precision about the experience. Around the end of the century, as Kenneth

---

[10] *Baptist Magazine*, July 1810, p. 392.
[11] *Baptist Magazine*, January 1850, p. 29.
[12] M. C. Bickersteth, *A Sketch of the Life and Episcopate of the Right Reverend Robert Bickersteth, D. D., Bishop of Ripon, 1857–1884*, London, 1887, p. 48.

Brown has shown, there was a declining readiness to refer to conversion among Congregationalists, even those in the ministry.[13] Yet for most of the century, and still at its end among most Baptists and Evangelical Anglicans, a sense of having made a definite entry on the way of holiness was *de rigeur*.

A second characteristic of the holy life was that it focused on the cross. The whole gospel sprang from the atonement. Robert Bickersteth opened his ministry with a sermon on 1 Corinthians 2:2: 'For I determined not to know any thing among you, save Jesus Christ and him crucified.' Bickersteth showed, his son noted, 'how every doctrine necessary to salvation centred around the Cross'.[14] Although that was pre-eminently true of justification, the first putting right of the soul with God, it was also true of sanctification, its growth in holiness. George Rogers, the Congregationalist who was senior tutor at the Pastor's College founded by C. H. Spurgeon, said exactly the same: 'The cross is the centre of our system.'[15] Consequently the doctrine of the atonement was related to the battle with sin that, according to the Calvinist, had to be waged throughout life. Andrew Fuller wrote a treatise on 'The Backslider', the believer who has fallen back into sin after making some progress on the Christian journey. One inducement to returning to the paths of righteousness was the mercy of God revealed in the cross. Fuller puts the words of Archbishop Cranmer in the mouth of the repentant backslider:

> Thou didst not give thy Son unto death for little sins only; but for all the greatest sins of the world; so that the sinner returns to thee with his whole heart, as I do here at this present.[16]

---

[13] K. D. Brown, *A Social History of the Nonconformist Ministry in England and Wales, 1800–1830*, Oxford, 1988, pp. 51–3.

[14] Bickersteth, *Bickersteth*, p. 39.

[15] *Outline of the Lord's Work by the Pastor's College and its Kindred Organisations at the Metropolitan Tabernacle*, London, 1867, p. 13.

[16] A. G. Gunton, ed., *The Complete Works of the Rev. Andrew Fuller*, London 1832, vol. 5, p. 513.

It was for the sake of Christ crucified that forgiveness was consistently available. This was the bedrock of continuing Christian discipleship.

The Bible, thirdly, was the supreme source of nurture in the spiritual life. Fuller's first remedy for backsliding was clear:

> Embrace every possible season of retirement for reading the holy Scriptures, especially those parts which are suited to thy case; and accompany it with prayer. – God's word hid in the heart is not only a preservative from sin, but a restorative from it.[17]

Conversely, however, Fuller held that habits of righteousness were fostered by the Bible. 'The more we read the holy Scriptures,' he wrote, 'the more we shall imbibe their spirit and be formed by them as a model.'[18] Bible reading, morning and evening, was the expected daily discipline. Agnes Campbell, the wife of a Congregational pastor in London, was said to have risen regularly to study it at 6 a.m. in winter and 5 a.m. in summer. In a study of the obituaries of one hundred women from each of the main Nonconformist denominations between 1825 and 1875, Linda Wilson has discovered that these obituaries very frequently quote from the Bible or mention Bible-reading in relation to their subjects. Among Congregationalists, 57 per cent refer to the practice; among Baptists, 33 per cent. Because of their greater leisure, especially among the middle classes from whom the Congregationalists were disproportionately drawn, women could in many cases turn to the Bible more readily than men. That perhaps accounts for the equivalent male samples being, for Congregationalists, 23 per cent and, for Baptists, 18 per cent.[19] Although both these figures are lower than their counterparts for women, they are nevertheless quite high when it is borne in mind that the obituaries were often brief.

---

[17] Ibid., p. 508.

[18] Ibid., p. 524.

[19] L. Wilson, 'Female Spirituality amongst Nonconformists, 1825–75', PhD dissertation, Cheltenham and Gloucester College of Higher Education, 1997, pp. 67–8, 136.

Even if some of these passages are merely expressing what their readers expected to hear about their subjects, the results are significant. Bible reading was obviously regarded as the heart of devotional practice.

Fourthly, a round of ceaseless activity was the crucial test of spiritual health. The essential motive for busyness was evangelism. Mary Cowell made her full decision for Christ when she was about eighteen in roughly 1838, subsequently joining Old Sampford Baptist Church.

> Having herself tasted that the Lord is gracious [ran her obituary] it became henceforth her aim to seek to lead others to that fountain of living waters whose healing efficacy she had herself experienced.[20]

Zeal for souls was a constant spur to action. Sunday, with its several services, prayer meetings, Sunday school sessions and more, provided the maximum opportunities. Hence, paradoxically, the sabbath day of rest became for Jane Lewis, another Baptist, from Diss in Norfolk, 'a day of incessant labour'.[21] The greatest effort was expected of those in the ministry. Charles Bridges wrote the standard pastoral handbook for Evangelical Anglican clergy in the first half of the nineteenth century.

> This general view [he concluded one section] of the principles of the pastoral work will show at once its laboriousness, and its importance. To acquaint ourselves with the various wants of our people; to win their affections; to give a seasonable warning, encouragement, instruction, or consolation; to identify ourselves with their spiritual interests, in the temper of Christian sympathy, and under a sense of Ministerial obligation; to do this with the constancy, seriousness, and fervid energy which the matter requires, is indeed a work of industry, patience and self-denial.[22]

---

[20] *Baptist Magazine*, August 1850, p. 500.
[21] *Baptist Magazine*, 1864, p. 692.
[22] C. Bridges, *The Christian Ministry*, 3rd edn, London, 1830, p. 477.

It was considered surprising that when Bickersteth took up his episcopal duties, he voluntarily chose to preach three times on Sundays.[23] And William Barlow, who, as vicar of Islington from 1887 to 1901 was at the busy hub of the Evangelical Anglican world, was said to have become 'old and bent before his time'.[24] The Evangelical conception of holiness did not foster retreat from the bustle of life except for temporary refreshment: contemplation was not its ideal. It was high praise to describe a layman as a Christian *worker*. Activism was a marked feature of the movement.

So the holy life among Evangelicals had four fundamental parameters: it opened with conversion, it was sustained by the power of the cross, it was fed by reading the Bible, and it issued in vigorous activity. Yet there were many other aspects of Evangelical spirituality within the Reformed tradition during the nineteenth century that deserve notice. In particular, because Evangelicalism was so closely bound up with the legacy of the Enlightenment, it reflects many of its characteristics. First and foremost it echoed the rationality of the Enlightenment. In contrast with High Churchmen, the movement was little attracted to symbol; instead Evangelicals were much preoccupied with the word, whether spoken, sung or written. The sermon was the centre of Evangelical worship. Although the sacraments were not neglected, they were not exalted, as they were by the Oxford Movement. Sermons were expected to inspire and nourish the spiritual life. Particularly on special occasions, they could attain an extraordinary length. One C.M.S. annual sermon, in 1832, lasted one and three-quarter hours.[25] Hymns were likewise valued for their doctrinal content, and not just for their rousing tempo. Isaac Watts was still the favourite hymnwriter of Calvinist Evangelicals, Churchmen as well as Dissenters. They insisted throughout the century, with few exceptions, that hymnody must be

---

[23] Bickersteth, *Bickersteth*, p. 153.
[24] F. J. Chavasse, 'Introduction', in M. Barlow, ed., *The Life of William Haggar Barlow, D.D.*, London, 1910, pp. xvi–xvii.
[25] By Edward Bickersteth, uncle of Robert. See E. Stock, *The History of the Church Missionary Society*, London, 1899, vol. 1, p. 262.

congregational, and not merely choral, so that all could sing the words with understanding. And books remained a staple of the devotional life. Philip Doddridge's *Rise and Progress of Religion in the Soul* (1745) was still a staunch favourite long into the nineteenth century. Parish libraries were founded by Evangelical clergy, boxes of books were circulated among impoverished Dissenting ministers, and periodicals with edifying contents proliferated. All were designed to stimulate the mind, for this was a cerebral form of religion.

Another Enlightenment characteristic was pragmatism. The firm adherence to principles of church order, whether of church or meeting house, that had marked the seventeenth century seemed less important as Evangelicals considered how best to evangelise the world. Maximum efficiency was their aim, and so they were prepared to co-operate with others who did not share their ecclesiology. They typically did not use ecclesiastical structures at all, but applied business methods outside them. The whole missionary enterprise was run by organisations based on the principles of the joint stock company. As C. R. Sumner, the Evangelical bishop of Winchester, put it in a sermon preached before the C.M.S. in 1828, 'religious charities . . . must be directed by calculation, and not by enthusiasm'.[26] Societies organised in this way for service at home and abroad mushroomed during the century. Evangelical Anglican and interdenominational philanthropic and religious institutions in London alone increased in number to 225 by 1827 and, in 1877, to an extraordinary 807.[27] Their annual gatherings in the Exeter Hall, the so-called May Meetings, were a remarkable demonstration of Evangelical strength. The growth of these bodies had a clear effect on the personal Christian life.

---

[26] *Proceedings of the Church Missionary Society*, vol. 12, p. 14, quoted by W. J. C. Ervine, 'Doctrine and Diplomacy: Some Aspects of the Life and Thought of the Anglican Evangelical Clergy, 1797–1837', PhD dissertation, University of Cambridge, 1979, p. 290.

[27] Edward Garbett at the Islington Clerical Meeting, 1877. *Record*, 19 January 1877.

A large proportion [ran the annual letter of the Baptist Union in 1837] of the leisure which heretofore might have been occupied in private religious exercises, is now spent in the service of our benevolent institutions.[28]

Bureaucratic involvement reinforced the natural activism of Evangelicals, turning them further from quiet devotion to public responsibilities. Faithful participation in organisations figured increasingly prominently in their obituaries as the century grew older. The pious life often became an institutional life.

A further feature of the Enlightenment's influence over religion was its encouragement of moralism. The more liberal expressions of Latitudinarian religion were notably moral in tone, humanitarian in action. Evangelicals, it is true, were wary of this moralising approach in that they insisted that religion must not be reduced to ethics. Too many layfolk had been lulled by moral essays delivered from Georgian pulpits into a mistaken sense that they met the requirements of the divine law without any radical change of heart. Yet Evangelical preaching was itself highly ethical. Duty faith injected moral obligation into the heart of religion. Against the antinomian tendencies that have been sketched, Evangelicals insisted on the divine commands to live uprightly. Preaching needed to be 'more a thing . . . of the conscience', declared John Angell James, probably the best known Congregational minister of the earlier nineteenth century.[29] Evangelicals were gratified when the home was moralised under Christian influence. Thus in the Evangelical parish of St George's, Southwark, a little girl carried home a text from a church school: 'Let all things be done decently and in order.' The rector, William Cadman, was highly gratified to learn that, according to the child's mother, 'it had been the means of

---

[28] *Account of the Proceedings of the Twenty-Fifth Annual Session of the Baptist Union, held in London, May 1, 2, 3, & 4, 1837*, London, [1837], p. 28.

[29] J. A. James to Dr Fletcher, 2 November 1840, in R. W. Dale, *The Life and Letters of John Angell James*, London, 1861, p. 283.

keeping her room tidy and clean'.[30] The Christian home, sacralised by family prayers, was a bastion of Evangelical spirituality. But moralising influences were carried into the whole of society. The battery of Evangelical organisations embraced much beside evangelism in their aims. The anti-slavery movement and the factory campaign for limiting hours at work were famously Evangelical in inspiration. Charles Bridges, in his clerical handbook, commended 'our Lord's example in combining kindness to the body with love to the soul'.[31] The Enlightenment principle of benevolence was a lodestar of the Evangelical movement.

Another characteristic of Evangelical religion associated with the Enlightenment was optimism. The doctrine of providence figured largely in the Evangelical mind. The Almighty was directing history, in its particular occurrences as well as in its general drift, towards his predetermined goal. There was therefore every reason for confidence in the future. A doctrine more intimately bound up with Enlightenment optimism pointed in the same direction. This was postmillennialism, the expectation of a time of peace and prosperity on the earth before the second advent, to be ushered in by the gospel. Thus in 1815 William Dealtry, rector of Clapham, drew attention to

> the unexampled diffusion of the holy scripture . . . the labours of Missionary Institutions . . . the anxiety of nations, hitherto involved in the darkness of superstition and idolatry, to come to the light of the gospel.

These phenomena seemed to indicate 'the dawning of that better day, which cheered the heart of the patriarch, and lighted up the vision of the prophet'.[32] The better day that was

---

[30] L. E. Shelford, *A Memorial of the Rev. William Cadman, M.A.*, London, 1899, p. 45.

[31] Bridges, *Christian Ministry*, p. 472.

[32] W. Dealtry, *A Sermon preached at the Parish Church of St Ann's, Soho, on Friday, May 5, 1815 before the London Society for promoting Christianity amongst the Jews, in the Seventh Year of their Establishment*, London, 1815, p. 17.

dawning was the millennium. Gradually as the century advanced, postmillennialism blended with the secular idea of progress. It nevertheless continued to provide religious sanction for the popular Victorian belief that society was steadily improving. Just as society was progressing under divine guidance, so should the individual. The popular understanding of personal sanctification fitted readily into the same mould. A Christian version of the secular doctrine of self-help was current. There should be a steady advance in personal devotion, in prayer, appreciation of the Bible and commitment to religious work. Spiritual improvement in the denominations stemming from the Reformed tradition was conceived as a matter of gradual attainment through human effort. Actual holiness was something, according to the great Baptist preacher C. H. Spurgeon, that 'we progressively manifest in our hearts and lives'.[33] It was an optimistic view of the spiritual life.

These, then, were some of the striking features of Evangelical spirituality in the bodies inheriting a Calvinist faith. They were congruent with much in the earlier Reformed approach to sanctification – it had always been bookish and had called for exertion in the quest for holiness – but they were given a fresh twist by the traits of the eighteenth-century cultural setting in which Evangelicalism was born. The Enlightenment legacy, however, was not just formative for the Evangelical Calvinist mode of understanding. The leaven of the Enlightenment permeated the lump of Evangelicalism more and more as time went by. It began to erode the distinctively Calvinistic elements with which it had earlier been associated. Thus William Jay, the distinguished Congregational minister at Bath during the first half of the nineteenth century, deliberately avoided any statement of theological system from the pulpit. This avoidance was a consequence of the distrust of metaphysics typical of the Enlightenment temper. In his later years Jay

---

[33] C. H. Spurgeon, 'The Winnowing Fan' (10 July 1870), *Twelve Sermons on Sanctification*, London, n. d., p. 265.

judged that, as a result, he had been deficient in doctrine.[34] He himself possessed a Calvinist framework of belief; but he failed to transmit it to his hearers. Likewise James Acworth, principal of Horton Baptist Academy, near Bradford, from 1835 to 1863, was said to be

> impatient of system and formulas. 'Make your own system' was his unvarying counsel to his men. He seldom or never gave Theological Lectures. His one aim and desire was that his pupils should read and understand 'The Word', or, as he loved to say, 'The Words of God'.[35]

Acworth's students emerged as Evangelicals, biblicist to the core, but rarely as Calvinists. The sapping of Calvinism from within the Evangelical tradition was carried out most thoroughly by the American revivalist Charles Finney. Through his writings from the 1830s and through his presence from 1849 to 1851, Finney exerted a powerful influence in England. He held that conversion was 'within the sinner's will' and therefore need never be delayed a moment. The gospel must no longer be obscured by the 'false philosophy' of the past. It was ridiculous, Finney claimed, for the Westminster Confession embodying Reformed teaching to set the standard of belief in the nineteenth century. It erects, he declared, 'a dead Pope'. His confidence in the Enlightenment 'spirit of enquiry' led him to abandon the Reformed tradition altogether.[36] Many in England heeded Finney because his methods seemed to increase the number of conversions. Under pressures such as these, Calvinism fell into decay in the later Victorian years.

Calvinism was also affected by the currents of Romantic sentiment. This was the cultural mood that, as we saw in the last chapter, had so significant a place in moulding High

---

[34] R. W. Dale, *The Old Evangelicalism and the New*, London, 1889, p. 12.
[35] W. Medley, *Rawdon Baptist College: Centenary Memorial*, London, 1904, p. 26.
[36] C. G. Finney, *Lectures on Systematic Theology*, ed. G. Redford, London, 1851, pp. vii, xi, viii.

Church spirituality. Its effects on Evangelical Calvinism came later and were less immediately transforming, yet they were to prove important in the long run. A key text was *The Divine Life in Man* (1859) by James Baldwin Brown, minister of Claylands Independent Church in London. His central doctrine was the Fatherhood of God. The Evangelical Calvinism of Fuller, he argued, was mistaken in bringing to the fore the role of God as governor of the universe, dispensing public justice. That, claimed Baldwin Brown, was to see the Almighty as operating according to rules, a mechanistic view – which, we might add, was conceived in the Enlightenment manner. On the contrary, Baldwin Brown insisted, God was personal, dealing with humanity on the basis of love, not of justice. He was the loving Father of all. Similar views were being expressed by Broad Church theologians in the Church of England who were following the lead of F. D. Maurice. Such opinions were not acceptable to traditionalists. On behalf of Evangelical Anglicans, J. C. Ryle, later bishop of Liverpool, contended in the following year that, according to the Bible, God is the Father of believers only.[37] Nevertheless the more liberal theological programme set out by Baldwin Brown, Maurice and their disciples steadily advanced during the rest of the century. By 1899 the *Evangelical Free Church Catechism*, representing all the major Free Church denominations, was issued describing God primarily as Love and as Father.[38] The milder image of God fostered a more relaxed spirituality. Feelings, not beliefs, were increasingly regarded as the test of Christian allegiance. Dogma was played down; response to the parental care of God was what mattered. Already in 1886 at the annual conference of the men trained at the Pastors' College, Spurgeon's highly conservative theological seminary, Charles Joseph, Baptist minister at Cambridge, was able to lecture on 'The Influence of Feeling upon Faith'.[39] One of the most critical hearers complained that the paper was an attack

---

[37] *Record*, 16 January 1860, p. 3.
[38] *An Evangelical Free Church Catechism for Use in Home and School*, London, 1899, p. 7.
[39] *Freeman*, 14 May 1886, p. 309.

on the authority of Scripture. That, however, was by no means
Joseph's intention. Rather, he was taking account of the
growing emphasis on feeling that was part of the Romantic
spirit of the age. The pendulum was swinging away from
precise doctrine and towards accommodating sensibility, even
among Evangelicals.

The host of the Pastors' College Conference, Charles
Haddon Spurgeon, was the man who most obviously stood
out against the trend. Spurgeon was a doughty champion of
Reformed doctrine who feared that contemporary tendencies
in theological opinion threatened to deprive the pulpit of its
gospel. In 1887–88 he protested against the 'Down Grade' in
doctrine that he saw around him. When the Baptist Union
refused to act against false teaching, he resigned from the
organisation in a great furore. Spurgeon was not, as has often
been supposed, leading an assault on Arminianism in defence
of the Reformed faith. He praised Wesley and had a Methodist
occupy his pulpit. Rather, he was rejecting the theological
reformulation in a Romantic pattern undertaken by men such
as Baldwin Brown. He was attacking the insidious effects of
what in 1876 he had called modern culture, intellectual
preaching and aesthetic taste.[40] Too many preachers were
following the fashions of the day and so renouncing the heart
of the gospel. 'Highly cultured soul-murderers,' he declared
with typical trenchancy, 'will find their "culture" to be no
excuse in the day of judgement.'[41] Ministers were trying to
pander to the tastes of richer congregations, giving them
literary essays rather than stirring sermons. Spurgeon saw
himself as standing for the common man against those with
social pretensions who would rob him of soul-saving truth.

Spurgeon's analysis was a penetrating one. The masses of
the ordinary people in late Victorian England were deeply
imbued with the form of Evangelical religion in an
Enlightenment mode that has been described in the present
chapter. The elite, as we saw in the last one, was more
susceptible to the rising tide of Romantic feeling. By the 1880s,

----

[40] *The Sword and the Trowel*, July 1876, p. 306.
[41] C. H. Spurgeon, *Lectures to My Students*, London, 1954, p. 208.

that tide was beginning to sweep along some of those in the Evangelical Calvinist tradition as well as the High Churchmen. In sophisticated urban and suburban congregations, ministers catered for the preferences of their hearers. They cited writers such as Carlyle and Ruskin and quoted poets such as Wordsworth and Tennyson. Upward social mobility was adding to the numbers who looked for such fare, while the cult of respectability reinforced the demand. Congregations wanted to preen themselves on being aware of the latest intellectual fashions. But ministers, according to Spurgeon, should not be 'the lackeys of those who affect gentility or boast refinement'.[42] Instead they should turn to the uncorrupted common people. The working classes were still hungry for the gospel and it should be given them without stint. That is what nearly all the men trained at Spurgeon's college proceeded to do during their ministerial careers. Spurgeon's stand did much to prolong the conservative Evangelical tradition into the following century.

In the twentieth century, however, the trends that Spurgeon resisted redoubled their force. The Romantic cultural style spread. What had previously been confined largely to the elite became the possession of a substantial proportion of the population. There was an increasing demand for spirituality to have a Romantic packaging. In the Church of England, Evangelical congregations called for more elaborate liturgy in imitation of the High Church party. In Nonconformity, especially Congregationalism, there was more teaching in the manner of Baldwin Brown. Evangelicalism was subject to twin pressures, to become both higher and broader. Eventually, in the 1920s, there was a partial separation. Organisations previously spanning the full range of Evangelical positions had to choose between liberal and conservative paths. Thus, for example, the Student Christian Movement took the liberal road whereas the London City Mission followed the conservative path. By contrast with America, where the modernist/fundamentalist split went deeper, there was no total bifurcation in England, but there was certainly a

---

[42] Ibid., p. 21.

tendency to diverge.[43] The effect was profoundly weakening for the Evangelical movement as a whole, which reached its nadir around the start of the Second World War.

For most of the nineteenth century, however, there had been a high degree of homogeneity in the Evangelical Calvinist world. Spirituality revolved round the Evangelical preoccupations of conversion, cross, Bible and activism; but it was also moulded by the rational approach, the pragmatic technique, the moralistic temper and the optimistic spirit of the Enlightenment. The Enlightenment had equally stamped its mark on society at large. The Victorian age was deeply coloured by rational, pragmatic values with a moral tone; and the prevalence of the idea of progress made it supremely optimistic. For a while the form of Evangelical religion met the needs of its host culture. The piety of the Evangelical movement was well designed to cater for the soul of Victorian England.

---

[43] The developments of the inter-war period are authoritatively covered in I. Randall, *Evangelical Experiences: A Study in the Spirituality of English Evangelicalism, 1918–1939*, Carlisle, 1999.

Chapter Three

The Wesleyan Tradition

The tradition of spirituality stemming from John Wesley effectively meant Methodism for most of the nineteenth century. It did not embrace the General Baptists, who, though Arminian in theology, did not share Wesley's distinctive teaching about holiness. By the end of the century there were a few groups outside Methodism, though springing from it, that also upheld the Wesleyan understanding. Of them the best known is the Salvation Army. But otherwise it was almost exclusively in the Methodist bodies that Wesleyan teaching flourished. This was true not only in the main Methodist denominations, the Wesleyans and the Primitives, but also in the Methodist New Connexion, the United Methodist Free Churches, the Bible Christians and even small fragments such as the Magic Methodists of Delamere Forest in Cheshire. Their appreciation of the holy life is the subject of this chapter.

The Methodists were distinguished from the Calvinist tradition by their espousal of Arminian theology. They rejected the Reformed doctrine of predestination according to which God took the initiative in choosing the elect for salvation. It was not that they rejected predestination altogether, since, after all, the idea was to be found in the Bible. Rather, they held that God had determined in advance to save any who freely responded to the gospel. Predestination was subordinate to future trust in Christ. The Redeemer died not just for the elect but, in accordance with a literal reading of the Scriptures, for all. Charles Wesley's hymns often insist on that point: 'For all, for all, my Saviour died.' The line is anti-Calvinist polemic. And if the Almighty did not decide in advance who would be saved, nor did he guarantee the ultimate salvation of those who were converted. Here was the teaching of the defectibility of faith: a person might possess saving faith and yet subsequently lose it. Real Christianity, according to Wesley, was entirely incompatible with sin. Hence any deliberate breach of the divine law destroyed the life of God in the soul. Thousands of individuals in the nineteenth century became believers in the Wesleyan manner, but then ceased to make a Christian profession. The century is littered with ex-Methodists such as the Chartist leader William Lovett. Consequently watchfulness about one's spiritual state was an essential element in Wesleyan piety. All believers had to beware lest they themselves became castaways.

Another feature of Wesley's teaching was his robust doctrine of assurance. This was his understanding of the witness of the Spirit. Anyone who was a Christian knew, from the work of the Spirit within, that he was in a state of grace. Here was the counterpart of the much stronger notion of assurance that emerged in the Calvinist tradition in the wake of Jonathan Edwards. In Methodism the teaching was peculiarly cherished. The 'direct witness of the Spirit' was celebrated as a principle for which Methodism had been raised up. That remained true even at the end of the nineteenth century. In 1903 George Jackson wrote about the witness of the Spirit in these terms:

> Our people are not, as a rule, quickly sensitive to differing shades of theological thought, and on some subjects it might be possible for a preacher to teach questionable doctrine without exciting any general alarm among his hearers; but a false note on this subject would be detected and resented at once. The joyful assurance of the favour of God is one of the chief marks of a Methodist.[1]

There were, as Jackson implies, direct effects on Methodist religious practice. When individuals first entered the experience, their exuberance was commonly infectious. Many chapels rang with the hallelujahs of new converts and their

---

[1] G. Jackson, *The Old Methodism and the New*, London, 1903, p. 43.

friends. It also made for vigorous singing. The magnificent body of Charles Wesley's hymnody was the glory of Methodism. It was sung with gusto, as its author intended, because it expressed the confidence of congregations that they had entered in by the strait gate. The certainty of heaven made for full-throated praise. Methodist spirituality was characteristically enthusiastic – what was called by a mid-century Methodist New Connexion publication 'an active, fervid, and joyous piety'.[2]

Yet it would be wrong to neglect the vast area of common ground between the Wesleyan and Calvinist traditions. Both were Evangelical, the one created by the Evangelical Revival, the other transformed by it. Hence Methodism, as much as the main Reformed groupings, bore the hallmarks of Evangelicalism. Methodist piety began with conversion. Perhaps it exalted the experience even more than the Calvinist variety. In a sample of mid-century obituaries for the Old Dissenters, conversion was mentioned in between 53 per cent (male Congregationalists) and 68 per cent (female Baptists); but the proportions among Methodists ranged from 83 per cent (male Wesleyans) to a remarkable 98 per cent (female Primitives).[3] Conversion was clearly of the utmost importance to the Methodist mind. The experience was urged by preachers in season and out of season. In 1874, for example, when travelling to Conference in Hull by train, a Primitive Methodist minister entered a compartment full of corn merchants and their clerks. 'Gentlemen,' he demanded, 'I wonder whether you are all converted?' There was an embarrassed rustling of newspapers until another Primitive who happened to be there declared, 'I don't know, sir, but I know I am.'[4] Generally, because of the witness of the Spirit,

---

[2] *The Jubilee of the Methodist New Connexion*, London, 1848, p. 398.

[3] L. Wilson, 'Female Spirituality amongst Nonconformists, 1825–75', PhD dissertation, Cheltenham and Gloucester College of Higher Education, 1997, pp. 56–8.

[4] J. Stephenson, *The Man of Faith and Fire: Or the Life and Work of the Rev. G. Warner*, London, 1902, p. 151.

Methodists were expected to know the precise time of their conversion. Yet it was accepted that some did not, and yet were real Christians. Instantaneous conversion was still being preached in some quarters in the late Victorian years, but it was widely felt that there were fewer instances than earlier in the century. There was now no insistence on any particular type of experience.[5] Conversion was now being watered down, but it was still looked for. The great change remained the opening of the spiritual life.

Christ crucified, as among the Calvinists, was the central devotional theme. A typical illustration comes from the obituary of Robert Simpson, a servant and Primitive Methodist class leader at Bavington in Northumberland. He was seized with inflammation of the bowels, and his wife told him the doctor could do no more:

> His reply was: 'Well,
>   "I the chief of sinners am,
>   but Jesus died for me;" '
> 'Yes', said she, 'the atonement.' He then fixed his eyes upon her, responding emphatically, 'Yes, he died, he died for me.'[6]

When John Rattenbury, one of the ablest Wesleyan preachers of the century, delivered the ordination sermon at the Conference of 1872, the burden of his message to the new ministers was that they should 'Preach the doctrines of the cross'.[7] While at a popular level the atonement remained the kernel of Methodist faith throughout the nineteenth century, there were signs before its end that a handful of more progressive thinkers were being influenced by the wave of incarnational theology that was noticed in the first chapter. In 1897 John Scott Lidgett, a rising Wesleyan minister, delivered the Fernley Lecture to Conference. It was published as *The Spiritual Principle of the Atonement*. Despite the title, the book

---

[5] Jackson, *Old Methodism and the New*, pp. 37–8.
[6] *Primitive Methodist Magazine*, January 1850, p. 61.
[7] H. O. Rattenbury, ed., *The Rev. John Rattenbury: Memorials*, London, 1884, p. 109.

followed the Anglican theologian F. D. Maurice in placing the greatest weight on the incarnation, not the atonement. There were complaints to the president of Conference, who upheld the view that Lidgett was wrong to make the shift of emphasis.[8] The centrality of the cross was still the official Wesleyan teaching. Methodist spirituality was nourished on the theme of the blood of Christ.

The Bible equally played a central part in shaping Methodist religious experience. An early nineteenth-century Wesleyan minister, John Smith, was said to have denied himself the indulgence of 'luxuriating in the riches of literary pleasures' for the sake of concentrating on the Bible.[9] A Bible Christian minister of the later part of the century, Samuel Pollard, was similarly devoted to Scripture:

> How he loved the Word of God his Bibles with their annotations plainly reveal. No duty, however important, was allowed to keep him from his daily practice of reading the Word, which he usually did on his knees.[10]

Nor was this attitude confined to ministers. T. B. Smithies, a mid-century Wesleyan layman who acted as editor of religious periodicals, made his convictions plain by the arrangement of his home. 'You could not enter into one of the rooms,' it was noticed, 'without seeing that the place of honour was given to the Bible.'[11] And the high value accorded the Bible went well down the social scale. At Cassington, Oxfordshire, in the 1870s, there was a female agricultural labourer whose work included turnip cleaning. She was a Primitive Methodist, and once remarked to a visiting preacher:

---

[8] J. S. Lidgett, *My Guided Life*, London, 1936, p. 157.
[9] R. Treffry, jun., *Memoirs of the Life, Character and Labours of the Rev. John Smith*, London, 1832, p. 93.
[10] W. J. Mitchell, *Brief Biographical Sketches of Bible Christian Ministers and Laymen*, Jersey, 1906, vol. 1, p. 43.
[11] G. S. Rowe, *T. B. Smithies (Editor of 'The British Workman'): A Memoir*, London, 1884, p. 72.

I likes the New Testament: you see it all so plain. I can understand what Paul, and Peter, and John says. It comes all over you, and makes you feel like – and then you cries, and then you larfs, and then you hollers!

The same travelling preacher came across a Primitive house-hold in a remote village whose members stuck pins in the family Bible to mark the promises: two or three thousand of them, perhaps twenty or thirty on the same page.[12] The Scriptures were not only paid lip service: such people put them to use.

Methodists, like their Evangelical Calvinist counterparts, were also activist. One Primitive Methodist minister, reviewing the year 1848, recorded that he had travelled, chiefly on foot, 3,484 miles; had made 1,790 family visits; and had preached about 400 times.[13] It was not only the obscurer men who drove themselves. John Rattenbury, as president of the Wesleyan Conference in 1871, preached between 400 and 500 sermons in the year.[14] '*Activity* for God,' declared the revivalist from America James Caughey, 'is a consequence of a healthy soul, as green to a healthy leaf.'[15] The range of activities is usefully illustrated by the obituary of Thomas Penrose, a Primitive minister who died in 1888:

Mr. Penrose was above everything else a man of *action*, whose hands were ever willing, and whose feet were ever ready, to do the great Master's bidding. . . He was filled with a burning zeal for the glory of his Saviour and the weal of his fellow-men, which was manifested in his indomitable perseverance in building chapels and schools, collecting large sums of money for this work; in promoting the cause of education; in sympathy and help for the poor, obtaining suitable situations for promising young men and women, and relief for suffering tradesmen; in his able advocacy of

---

[12] Stephenson, *Warner*, pp. 183, 184.

[13] *Primitive Methodist Magazine*, February 1850, p. 66.

[14] Rattenbury, *Rattenbury*, p. 50.

[15] J. Caughey, *Earnest Christianity Illustrated: Or Selections from the Journal of James Caughey*, London, 1857, p. 103.

the temperance cause; and in the active interest he took in all local movements for the welfare of those amongst whom he lived.[16]

Ordinary Methodists characteristically threw themselves into a full round of meetings. Chapel provided an enormous number of opportunities: prayer meetings and business meetings, visiting societies and tract societies, bazaars and sewing circles (for the women), and much else. The greater the involvement, as a general rule, the higher the piety rating with contemporaries. The spiritual life was an active life.

The likeness of Methodists to their Evangelical contemporaries in the Reformed tradition went even further. They shared not only the main features of Evangelicalism; they also shared the form in which Evangelicalism expressed itself. For Methodists, as for Evangelical Calvinists, their faith was moulded by the Enlightenment. John Wesley himself was an Enlightenment thinker.[17] It is true that he had a credulous side. As Henry Rack and others have shown, he identified with much of the superstitious dimension of popular culture.[18] Yet he held attitudes typical of the age of reason. He was an empiricist, believing in the investigation of religious experience. He appealed to the evidence drawn from this research to confute the metaphysics of the past. His method conformed to Newtonian norms, for it was strictly scientific. He explored the powers of electric current, especially for healing. And he shared the correct taste of the Georgian period, taking Jonathan Swift and Alexander Pope as the models of a plain and succinct style. He approved the chaste diction of Charles's hymns. John Wesley participated fully in the high culture of his age. Far from being a throwback to an obscurantist past, he was a man of (as he put it) 'reason and religion'.

---

[16] W. J. Brownson, et al., *Heroic Men: The Death Roll of the Primitive Methodist Ministry*, London, 1889, p. 305.

[17] F. Dreyer, 'Faith and Experience in the Thought of John Wesley', *American Historical Review*, vol. 88, 1983.

[18] H. D. Rack, *Reasonable Enthusiast: John Wesley and the Rise of Methodism*, London, 1989.

It is not surprising that Wesley's disciples aspired to follow in their master's wake. Many of them showed an equivalent respect for reason. Adam Clarke, the greatest intellectual of early nineteenth-century Methodism, was an advocate of Enlightenment values. The aim of the Christian, he urged, was 'to be in the *state of happiness*', that supreme goal of the age of reason – though true happiness, he contended, depended on the spiritual state.[19] A grand aim of Methodism was the spread of superior principles throughout the land. The masses of the population were to be civilised as well as evangelised. Methodists were as eager as Denis Diderot and his fellow promoters of the French *Encyclopaedia* to disseminate enlightened ideas. Here was much of the motivation for the Sunday school movement, which in its earlier years taught reading and writing as much as religion. The Methodist connexions operated vast publishing programmes. Individual Methodists, catching the vision, took up similar work independently. T. B. Smithies alone became editor of the *Band of Hope Review, British Workman, Children's Friend, Infant's Magazine, Friendly Visitor, Family Friend, Weekly Welcome* and *Band of Mercy Advocate*.[20] And the civilising mission proved remarkably successful. People acquired literacy, bought and read the magazines, distributed tracts themselves and used local preachers' libraries. A Wesleyan Association millhand with a large family to support, whose wages can hardly have been more than £30 a year, spent about £16 on purchasing Adam Clarke's biblical commentary.[21] Knowledge was highly prized. Methodism was a movement committed to the advance of reason.

It was also profoundly concerned with the Enlightenment principle of benevolence. There was, of course, a coincidence here between the views of the age of reason and traditional

---

[19] A. Clarke, 'Genuine Happiness the Privilege of Every Real Christian in This Life', *Discourses on Various Subjects*, vol. 1, London, 1828, p. 233.

[20] Rowe, *Smithies*, p. 55.

[21] *Wesleyan Methodist Association Magazine*, October 1853, p. 487.

Christian charity. But the schemes undertaken went far beyond the custom of almsgiving. In large towns there flourished a series of Stranger's Friend Societies, run by Methodists but catering for individuals of any or no religious profession. As time went by Methodists became involved in immense structures of organised philanthropy. The promotion of the social welfare of the people was a professed aim alongside evangelism. On occasion the two could appear to collide. Thus T. B. Smithies, an early teetotaller, was alarmed to discover at mid-century that nearly two-thirds of those in prison, many of them as a result of intoxication, had passed through Sunday school. He therefore urged in a pamphlet that Sunday school teachers should warn their charges of the dangers of strong drink. He was sharply criticised by other Wesleyans for implying that the gospel alone was not sufficient for the safety of the children. Temperance work was frowned on as a diversion from more strictly religious activities. Yet Smithies persevered in his anti-drink crusade for the rest of his career, and also took up other humanitarian causes: Ragged Schools for destitute children, assistance for released prisoners and the rescue of animals from cruelty.[22] The desire to improve the lot of fellow beings, even beyond the bounds of the human race, was sufficiently powerful to override the caution of others. Smithies was but one instance of involvement in the organised practical care for the needy that was common among nineteenth-century Methodists. The imperative to good works, reinforced by the moralism of the Enlightenment, was widely heeded.

Pragmatism, too, was as much a feature of Methodism as of Calvinist Evangelicalism. Methodist apologists justified their connexional machinery on precisely this ground. Their polity was not (as among Independents) deduced from Scripture or (as among High Churchmen) from tradition. It was simply argued that their organisation was the most efficient means of saving souls. Methodism therefore produced some entirely novel religious techniques. Some were controversial. In the first decade of the nineteenth century, for example, there was

---

[22] Rowe, *Smithies*, pp. 34, 38–40, 58, 63–5.

an attempt to transplant from America the outdoor festivals of preaching and prayer called camp meetings. The Wesleyan authorities forbade them; enthusiasts from near Stoke-upon-Trent went ahead; and the innovators ended up creating a whole fresh denomination, the Primitive Methodists. Other methods were standard features of all the connexions during the century. One was the class meeting, a weekly gathering of society members for mutual encouragement in spiritual progress. Their effectiveness varied with the quality of the leadership. Classes were useful for Christian nurture when their leaders were eager to improve the standard of holiness of the attenders, when they were themselves capable in prayer and when they were conscientious in visiting absent members. The love-feast was another distinctive Methodist institution. Held quarterly in some larger societies but irregularly elsewhere, love-feasts were occasions for consuming bread and water but also, more importantly, events where members could bear open testimony to their spiritual experience. What was shared in relative privacy in the class meeting became public property at the love-feast. Both institutions declined in vigour and frequency as the century proceeded. But for much of the period they were effective vehicles for developing the spirituality of members.

Optimism, furthermore, was a hallmark of the Enlightenment that was also stamped on Methodism. The belief in human ability inherent in Arminianism has been seen by Bernard Semmel as a revolutionary shift towards an optimistic view of humanity.[23] The postmillennial teaching upheld by Calvinist Evangelicals was equally maintained in the Wesleyan tradition. At the end of the century, although its firm dogmatic outlines had faded, postmillennialism was still treated by a knowledgeable Methodist minister as 'our' doctrine.[24] Mark Guy Pearse, one of the broadest-minded ministers in the later Victorian years, merged the hope of the millennium into the secular idea of progress. 'He had a firm

---

[23] B. Semmel, *The Methodist Revolution*, London, 1974.
[24] I. E. Page, ed., *John Brash: Memorials and Correspondence*, London, 1912, p. 185.

belief,' according to his biographers, 'that the world was getting better.'[25] Here was a strain of confident hope for the future. But the greatest sign of optimism was the distinctive Methodist teaching about holiness. Wesley had concluded that a state of entire sanctification, which he preferred to call perfect love, was available on earth. He had discovered too many instances of full salvation to doubt it. Calvinists might demur, holding that the struggle against sin could never be over before death, but nineteenth-century Methodists inherited from their founder the belief that a variety of holiness fit for heaven was attainable in this life. There was a ground for optimism about human potential that took them far beyond the Reformed position.

Entire sanctification as embodied in the nineteenth-century Wesleyan tradition is therefore worth lingering over. It was a deeply populist style of holiness. In 1857 William Braimbridge, a Free Methodist minister, held a series of revival meetings in the village of South Somercotes in Lincolnshire. On Sunday morning he preached on sanctification and in the afternoon a fellowship meeting turned into a prayer meeting for the blessing.

> O how readily were the long forms filled, and with tears, sobs, and groans, were many cries made to God for holiness of heart! The power did come, melting, softening and wounding. One young woman with cries and bitterness of spirit exclaiming, 'O what anguish of soul do I feel,' panted, breathed and prayed; soon by faith she seized the prize, joy sprung up in her heart; instantly she arose on her feet, clapped her hands, and cried, 'I've got the blessing. I'm happy, I'm happy!'[26]

In this case the experience was a result of teaching on the subject; it was gained in a communal context; and it was fostered by revivalism. All these features, though by no means universal, were typical. What were the other main characteristics of this species of holiness?

---

[25] Mrs G. Unwin and J. Telford, *Mark Guy Pearse: Preacher, Author, Artist*, London, 1930, p. 233.
[26] *Revivalist*, May 1857, p. 75.

In the first place, for much of the century entire sanctification normally came after a long quest. It is true that it was held that the experience could arrive at the same time as conversion or shortly afterwards; but there was usually a protracted delay. Thus an early Primitive Methodist woman at Snaith in Yorkshire was said to have 'long thirsted' for full salvation before she secured it in 1822.[27] A Primitive minister obtained it in 1855 only after ardently seeking it for two full years.[28] Even at the crisis point, release was not automatic. The Wesleyan T. B. Smithies, though active in a mission led by James Caughey at York in the 1840s, spent three hours in 'intense earnestness of pleading' before attaining it.[29] There was much scope for self-reproach.

> Why have I not got it? [asked a Primitive minister in a letter] Why have I not had it long ago! Why? Because I have been unworthy, so unfaithful, and have not watched and prayed as I ought to have done. May God forgive me! May I be enabled to believe for the fulness of this heavenly blessing![30]

Pressing after holiness, the attitude that was urged on Methodists once they were converted, did not mean that they reached the goal rapidly.

The experience, secondly, was to be obtained by faith. Here was a sharp contrast with the Reformed tradition, according to which unremitting effort was called for. Holiness, in the teaching of Calvinists such as Fuller, could be achieved only by dint of regular deeds that hardened into godly habits. But in the Wesleyan tradition, sanctification, like justification, was not of works but of faith. Samuel Hick was a West Riding blacksmith who had one sermon published in 1831 in an orthography that attempted to reproduce his Yorkshire accent. The subject was entire sanctification. Some seek

[27] *Primitive Methodist Magazine*, July 1924, p. 156.
[28] Stephenson, *Warner*, p. 47.
[29] Rowe, *Smithies*, p. 32.
[30] S. Morris, *Memorials of the late Rev. George Bagley*, London, 1860, p. 10.

holiness, Hick asserted, in the wrong way, through watching their eyes, ears and tongues – forgetting their hearts. We receive justification not by deeds of the law but by prayer and faith. 'Ye mun it same way,' he went on, 'rassall, an prae, an *beleev*, at ya ma obtaine this blessing ov a klean hart.'[31] The experience, confirmed the much more sophisticated Mark Guy Pearse in 1865, was received 'by simple faith'.[32]

Consequently, thirdly, perfect love was available only through a crisis equivalent to conversion. It was a revolutionary change of character. True, there was a gradual process, beginning at conversion, of the mortification of sin in the soul. But sanctification arrived in an instant. Adam Clarke remarked that in the Bible purification, like pardon, was not a matter of graduation.[33] When T. B. Smithies found the experience, he told a friend that 'it won't do to try to grow into a clean heart'.[34] Sanctification was a decisive stage in the Christian pilgrimage.

Yet, fourthly, sanctification, like justification, was a possession that could be lost. Faith was necessary to sustain it as well as to grasp it initially. Full salvation could be forfeited in a variety of ways. One Wesleyan Methodist Association minister lost it through not daring to testify to the experience.[35] An early Bible Christian lost it through reasoning over why he should be treated unkindly when he did testify to having received it.[36] A Primitive Methodist servant lost it 'through singing a song at the celebration of his old master's marriage'.[37] The effect of the lapse could be devastating, as for a Leeds Protestant Methodist: 'his confidence was shaken, darkness clouded his soul, and for three days he continued to struggle against unbelief'.[38] There

---

[31] S. Hick, *Entire Sanctification: A Sermon*, Barnsley, 1831, p. 15.
[32] Unwin and Telford, *Pearse*, p. 38.
[33] Cited in *Revival Miscellanies . . . selected from the Works of the Rev. James Caughey*, London, n. d., p. 18.
[34] Rowe, *Smithies*, p. 333.
[35] *Wesleyan Methodist Association Magazine*, March 1853, p. 138.
[36] *Arminian Magazine*, August 1822, p. 245.
[37] *Primitive Methodist Magazine*, June 1850, p. 383.
[38] *United Methodist Free Churches Magazine*, July 1858, p. 377.

could be a prolonged period in which the experience was lost and regained over and over again. There was no more guarantee of eternal security for the sanctified than for the justified.

Fifthly, there were perceptible results in the spiritual life. Entire sanctification often renewed the zeal kindled at the start of Christian discipleship. 'I feel tonight,' said one newly sanctified Primitive class leader, 'as I have not felt since my conversion.'[39] Prayer was revitalised. 'Oh,' commented a Primitive missioner, 'how these newly sanctified people prayed in a prayer meeting.'[40] A Primitive Methodist mother, having received purity of heart, regularly prayed in private seven or eight times a day.[41] Activism was equally reinforced. One man recently purified through holiness meetings in Hull was 'now going on in usefulness'.[42] The best workers in a Methodist society were commonly those claiming the experience. Although cases of hypocrisy abounded, it was expected that the state of holiness would produce fruit in secular affairs. Sanctification, it was recognised, should 'infuse a spirit of pure morality into the business transactions of life, so that every man's word should be his bond'.[43] And there was a necessary shunning of worldliness:

> those recreations [according to a holiness writer in 1872] which bring us into frequent contact with unconverted persons, are, to say the least, dangerous: they may promote physical gain; but will produce spiritual loss. And as for balls, masquerades, and midnight dances, it is impossible to reconcile them with being 'holy in all manner of conversation'.[44]

Novels, smoking and football were often cited as particular sources of temptation. Sanctification was not just a private

---

[39] Stephenson, *Warner*, p. 198.
[40] Ibid., p. 35.
[41] *Primitive Methodist Magazine*, February 1850, p. 124.
[42] Stephenson, *Warner*, p. 198.
[43] H. J. Staley, *Christ Our Sanctification*, London, 1872, p. 104.
[44] Ibid., pp. 101–2.

experience: it was expected that it would reap a harvest of righteousness too.

Perfection in love, then, was the jewel in the crown of the Wesleyan tradition. But it is important to appreciate that, like other understandings of holiness, it did not remain static. There were substantial changes in the tradition over time. In the first half of the century the formulation of John Wesley still prevailed. Wesley's *Plain Account of Christian Perfection* remained the main source of the idea. Thus John Hannah, from 1843 the first tutor at the Didsbury branch of the Wesleyan Theological Institution, did not diverge in his lectures from the teaching of Wesley.[45] Still in the 1850s the doctrine of holiness learned by a young man at Nottingham was 'exclusively that of John Wesley'.[46] But the pattern had already started to change.

The first significant repackaging of holiness teaching came through James Caughey, an American revivalist who toured England four times between 1841 and the mid-1860s. Caughey, a self-educated man, had operated in the same area as the celebrated Charles Finney. Just as Finney remodelled the Calvinist tradition in radical Enlightenment terms in order to maximise conversions, so Caughey remoulded the Wesleyan tradition. It was crucial, he believed, to encourage as many people as possible to enter the experience of sanctification. Applying common sense in the Enlightenment mode, he reasoned that faith was a voluntary act. Therefore individuals could choose to believe God's promises as soon as they became aware of them. The results of preaching this message were gratifying: at his missions there were nearly as many cases of sanctification as of conversion. Caughey differed from the traditional teaching in several respects. First, because he declared that there was no need to wait to be sanctified, the previous norm of agonised wrestling towards the experience was superseded. Secondly, there was no need for any

---

[45] J. Hannah, *Introductory Lectures on the Study of Christian Theology*, London, n. d., chaps 57–8.

[46] I. E. Page, *A Long Pilgrimage with Some Guides and Fellow Travellers*, London, 1914, p. 145.

confirming awareness of having received a new heart. Whereas in the past the witness of the Spirit was thought to be as essential to sanctification as to justification, now Caughey began to teach that the deliberate act of believing was enough to guarantee that holiness of heart had come. It was a matter of 'naked faith, stripped of all feeling'.[47] And thirdly, since long seeking and interior confirmation were unnecessary, purity of heart need no longer be confined to a small number of enlightened souls, but was available to the multitudes. Phoebe Palmer and her husband, further American revivalists who followed where Caughey had led, taught much the same. The doctrine of full salvation was being adapted, under Enlightenment influences, for mass consumption. The style of entire sanctification was being democratised.

Other processes, however, were transforming the experience in a totally different way. Sections of Wesleyanism in particular were becoming highly respectable. Greater prosperity was bringing higher standards of propriety in its train. There was a strong inducement to tone down the distinctive features of what outsiders might judge to be fanatical. Already in the 1830s Abraham Scott, a leading Wesleyan minister, when preaching before Conference on Christian sanctification, put the teaching in a definitely modified form. How, he asked, was purification to be obtained? Part of the answer was by not resisting the Spirit, by prayer and by faith in the blood; but another part was 'by a diligent and devout use of divine ordinances'.[48] Regular churchgoing, Bible reading and following Methodist ways formed the path of holiness. It was a formula suited to the years when Jabez Bunting was imposing institutional order on the connexion. The most influential recasting of the doctrine along these lines was by William Arthur, one of the secretaries of the Wesleyan Missionary Society, in his book, *The Tongue of Fire* (1856). He does urge his readers to embrace full salvation, but in blunted terms that make it hard to discover precisely what he is commending. By 1882, when George Osborn, then the

[47] Caughey, *Earnest Christianity Illustrated*, p. 152.
[48] A. Scott, *Christian Sanctification*, Hanley, n. d., p. 17.

dominant figure in Wesleyanism, preached a sermon at Conference, he merely mentioned that the Holy Ghost is 'competent to purify the heart continually by His indwelling, by His incessant operation'.[49] This was mild, milk-and-water teaching by comparison with the earlier tradition. No Calvinist could have taken offence at Osborn's phraseology. Rising respectability had toned down the official teaching on the subject.

A special twist to holiness teaching was given in the last two decades of the century by another Wesleyan, Hugh Price Hughes. Appointed head of the West London Mission in 1886, he had a passionate desire to show the relevance of Christianity to the social problems of the day. Accordingly, holiness was redefined as 'healthiness'. Hughes claimed that there was no point in tarrying for power from on high, since believers merely had to obtain more of what they already possessed. That was effectively to eliminate the crisis of sanctification. Christ, Hughes declared, received the anointing of the Holy Ghost 'by going on in the path of duty' and his followers should do the same.[50] They should see their responsibility to show mercy to the unfortunate in society. In Hughes's version, the contours of the doctrine were drastically eroded for the sake of meeting contemporary needs.

There was, furthermore, a tendency in the later nineteenth century to lose sight of the distinctive Methodist teaching on holiness altogether. Already in the 1850s there were many comments that the experience was much rarer than in the past. By the 1860s it was possible for *The Methodist New Connexion Magazine* to carry an article on 'The Law of Holiness' which showed no trace of the Wesleyan tradition whatsoever.[51] Individual society members were regarded as 'saints', and referred to as such in their obituaries, without any crisis of personal sanctification. A future Primitive Methodist president of Conference showed from the pulpit in the 1870s that the Methodist doctrine of entire sanctification was simply

---

[49] *King's Highway*, November 1882, p. 380.
[50] *King's Highway*, September 1886, pp. 303, 318.
[51] *Methodist New Connexion Magazine*, October 1866, pp. 612–14.

wrong. His text was 1 Kings 8:46: 'For there is no man that sinneth not.'[52] The tradition was in an advanced state of decay.

It was in these circumstances that there was a resurgence of the belief and practice of entire sanctification – the holiness revival of the later nineteenth century. In 1872 a group of four Wesleyan ministers founded a periodical, *The King's Highway*, to propagate full salvation. From 1885 the annual Southport Convention became a centre for the spread of the same message. Holiness was resuscitated as a class meeting theme. Special gatherings were held in many circuits, often midweek afternoon meetings for ladies.[53] How did this renewal take place? It was partly because of literature and speakers from America, where the holiness movement had taken off in the wake of the Civil War. It was partly because it was backed by prosperous laymen, notably Cuthbert Bainbridge, of the family owning the Newcastle department store of that name, who initially paid for *The King's Highway*. But another factor was the cultural setting: holiness was being recast in a Romantic mould.

The debt of the new holiness impulse to Romanticism is evident in little details. From the start, for example, fresh flowers appeared at the Southport Convention.[54] *The King's Highway* was willing to recommend authors from the past beloved of the High Churchmen of Romantic sensibility: Jeremy Taylor, Catherine of Siena and even Thomas Aquinas.[55] The intellectual influences show the same affinities. John Brash, the brains of the movement, was swayed by F. D. Maurice and Horace Bushnell, the chief American Congregationalist to have embraced a liberal theology of Romantic hue. Brash was even drawn to pantheism at one stage.[56] Here were

---

[52] Stephenson, *Warner*, p. 165.

[53] *King's Highway*, June 1886, pp. 206–7.

[54] *To the Uttermost: Commemorating the Diamond Jubilee of the Southport Methodist Holiness Convention, 1885–1945*, London, 1945, p. 16.

[55] Ibid., September 1872, p. 303; January 1882, pp. 12–16; February 1872, p. 42.

[56] Page, ed., *Brash*, pp. 10, 48.

definite Broad Church sympathies. The Romantic tone is evident supremely in the way the leaders expressed the doctrine. There was a vagueness that would have been shunned in the past. *The King's Highway* warned its readers to avoid 'rigidly defined views of this experience'.[57] Brash was criticised by a defender of the older Methodist tradition for being 'very modern', meaning that he was not sufficiently definite. Brash, in turn, found the literature coming from America 'very mechanical', his preference being to emphasise that holiness was 'living union with a living Saviour'.[58] There is the contrast between the older and the newer versions of the doctrine in a nutshell: the older style thought of human behaviour, in a way characteristic of the Enlightenment, as mechanical, machine-like; the newer style treated it, in the manner of Romanticism, as living, personal, organic. The Wesleyan tradition was being affected, after long delay, by the cultural mood that had given rise to the Oxford Movement.

Yet there remained a division of opinion within the holiness revival. The contrast of styles was evident in a dispute that raged around the nature of holiness in the last years of the century. When a person entered full salvation, was sin eradicated or not? If so, then a person could be said to enjoy a state of sinlessness. The older tradition, not seeing a problem in this area, had been happy to speak of sin being rooted out of the heart. This was still the position of many of the late Victorian champions of holiness within Methodism such as the evangelist Thomas Cook. It was also the position of the Pentecostal League of Prayer, founded by Reader Harris in 1891. But Brash found the Pentecostal League view (again) a 'very mechanical method', pointing out that Harris had been a mechanical engineer before he became a barrister.[59] Although, in deference to its constituency, *The King's Highway* often carried statements that sin was indeed eradicated, Brash was much more ambiguous in private. He did not accept a non-eradication theory, but nor did he embrace eradication:

---

[57] *King's Highway*, October 1873, p. 354.
[58] Page, ed., *Brash*, p. 38.
[59] Ibid., p. 55.

'Not only is the phrase unscriptural, but the figure is one that has no application to the case, and no correspondence to anything the Spirit does in the human heart.'[60] Brash was not alone in his reservations. Thomas Champness, for example, who spoke from the Southport platform, also rejected eradication.[61] Keswick, the subject of the next chapter, threw its weight in the balance against sinlessness, and its influence was felt in Methodism. The controversy on this subject was an indication of the tension between two different ways of expressing holiness teaching that were associated with distinct cultural ambiences.

The Romantic manner left its mark on Southport. W. H. Tindall, its founder, insisted on breadth of teaching in its early years, not excluding Champness or even Hughes. Significantly Tindall's own consecration took place at Keswick. But the Romantic mood, as we have seen, was attractive largely to the elite in the late nineteenth century. The broader version of the Wesleyan tradition does seem to have drawn in a few well-to-do individuals, notably James Wood, the owner of a Liverpool iron-foundry who gave the site for the Southport Convention. Methodism, however, was poorly represented in the national elite. So the Wesleyan tradition had almost no contact with the opinion-formers of English life. There was little scope for the Romantic recasting of entire sanctification to spread among them. The doctrine was known in early twentieth-century academic circles almost solely as a curiosity from the past in the writing of Newton Flew, the Cambridge Methodist scholar.[62] The Romantic form of Wesleyan holiness teaching failed to make headway.

The great bulk of the holiness constituency in late Victorian Methodism, like their counterparts in the Salvation Army, consisted of humble folk. The teaching of full salvation seems

---

[60] Ibid., p. 33.

[61] H. T. Smart, *The Life of Thomas Cook: Evangelist and First Principal of Cliff College, Calver*, London, 1913, pp. 280–1.

[62] N. Flew, *The Idea of Perfection in Christian Theology: An Historical Study of the Christian Ideal for the Present Life*, Oxford, 1934.

to have remained strongest in Yorkshire, among the farmers of the Dales and ordinary society members in the east of the county at places such as Scarborough, Beverley and Hull. These people were barely touched by novel cultural currents. They warmed more to Thomas Cook's sharply chiselled teaching about eradication than to John Brash's more equivocal formulations. Cook's *New Testament Holiness* (1902) became the popular handbook of entire sanctification for the new century. *The King's Highway*, with its more high-brow approach, did not survive to the end of the Victorian age. *Joyful News* became the voice of the movement. It was issued from Cliff College, in Derbyshire, where Cook was principal in the years before the First World War. Scriptural holiness became the concern of a limited and relatively proletarian sector within twentieth-century Methodism.

The Wesleyan tradition had been, from its origins, deeply imbued with Enlightenment values. Wesley himself was a distinguished theorist of the English Enlightenment, marrying Evangelical religion with the worldview of reason, science and experiment. Wesleyan spirituality remained bound up with rationality, moralism, pragmatism and optimism. The doctrine of entire sanctification fitted this pattern, the supreme evidence of the optimism of the Wesleyan approach: a person could be free from sin in this life. This doctrine was therefore susceptible to remodelling by the more radical Enlightenment method of James Caughey, with his promise of immediate divine response to a voluntary human act. It is true that Romantic sensibility did impinge on holiness teaching through the influence of John Brash and his circle in the last thirty years of the century. But the core members of the holiness movement preferred an older, more mechanical, understanding. They were still wedded to the eradicationist teaching of Thomas Cook that harked back to the Enlighten-ment. In the early twentieth century distinctively Wesleyan piety was confined to relatively small numbers and to people nearer the bottom than the top of the social scale. As Romantic influences continued to spread, the tradition did not have the ear of a wide public. It continued to satisfy the spiritual needs of a few in the smaller holiness bodies – the Pentecostal

League, the International Holiness Mission, the Calvary Holiness Church – and of some in the Salvation Army. But within Methodism, despite the witness of Cliff College, it stood apart from the denominational mainstream, seeming obscure and rather quirky. In the twentieth century the Wesleyan tradition was condemned to the margins of English religious life.

Chapter Four

The Keswick Tradition

The Keswick teaching about holiness was named after the town in the Lake District that became its chief centre. Each July thousands would throng to the holiday resort to attend a convention where guidance would be given on the path of consecration. The message was often summarised as sanctification by faith. That epitome, as we saw in the last chapter, was entirely congruent with Wesleyan doctrine. The formula reveals the affinity of the Keswick method with John Wesley's message of full salvation. Yet the teaching at the annual convention was upheld chiefly by people in the Calvinist tradition. They regularly insisted that sanctification by faith was compatible with Reformed distinctives. The convention aimed to overcome the difference between the two contrasting theological approaches. Keswick can best be understood as a synthesis of the subjects of the last two chapters.

Keswickers claimed a long tradition. They frequently referred to *The Gospel Mystery of Sanctification* (1692) as an authority for the teaching of holiness by faith within Reformed circles. The author of the book was Walter Marshall, a Presbyterian divine who was a fellow of New College, Oxford, during the Commonwealth. Subsequently he became vicar of Hursley in Hampshire, which, intriguingly, was to be the parish served by John Keble in the Victorian era. Marshall was ejected from his incumbency in 1662, and so became a Nonconformist. He died in 1680 and his book was issued posthumously. It does teach sanctification by faith, though the doctrine is not formulated as precisely as it was to be on the Keswick platform. Marshall's work is part of the semi-mystical strain in some of the later Puritans. There was no continuity between Marshall in the seventeenth century and Keswick in the nineteenth. No eighteenth-century writers were cited with similar approval at the convention. Here again is an instance of the nineteenth-century practice of inventing a tradition. Contemporary practice was being buttressed by evidence drawn selectively from a handful of earlier sources – or in this case from a single one. It would be wrong to speak of a Keswick tradition before the late nineteenth century. The 'tradition' in fact originated in the years around 1870.

Keswick nevertheless had a precursor in the spirituality of Mildmay. Conferences had been held, first at Barnet from 1856, and then at Mildmay Park in north London from 1864. They were organised annually by William Pennefather, who was successively incumbent of the two parishes. The themes each year were foreign and home missions, the second advent and holiness. Because the speakers were chosen personally by Pennefather, his preoccupations were stamped on the conference. He believed in particular that contemporary Christians neglected the work of the Holy Ghost. In the hymn for which he is probably now best remembered, 'Jesus stand among us', Pennefather wrote the lines, 'Breathe the Holy Spirit into every heart'. He inherited the intensely otherworldly piety of his upper middle-class home in Dublin. In those circles there arose the strong beliefs about the second advent that he subsequently maintained; and there, too, were the earliest stirrings of the Brethren movement. Pennefather was related by marriage to John Nelson Darby, the creator of the dispensationalist system of prophetic thought and the leader of the more extreme section of the so-called Plymouth Brethren. Although Pennefather repudiated their position, many of the Brethren attended the Mildmay conferences. Their common teaching of eternal sanctification played a part in its discussions. A Christian, on this view, was wholly sanctified in status at conversion; it only remained for that sanctification to be worked out in experience. This opinion played a part in the growing interest in holiness at Mildmay that Pennefather was delighted to foster. 'I never knew any one,' remembered a disciple, 'to whom it was given, as it was to him, to take men by the hand and lead them "into the Holiest" '.[1] Pennefather had contact with the town of Keswick. He visited T. D. Harford-Battersby, the vicar of St John's there, who was later to organise the convention. But Pennefather himself died in 1873, before the first gathering at Keswick.

The Mildmay conference outlived its founder. Indeed it grew in size after Pennefather's death, attracting nearly 3,000 attenders each year by the 1880s. It never, however, became a centre of the distinctive Keswick message. Opponents of Keswick teaching, as well as its advocates, were allowed to address the London meetings. Yet Pennefather had given a platform to the speakers who first spread the message of sanctification by faith beyond Methodism. The Mildmay conferences, furthermore, created a body of zealous Christian workers, already keen to hear addresses on holiness, that formed a natural constituency for the new views when they arrived. The Mildmay network provided connections for the early Keswick teachers. It was the fertile soil on which the seed of the new teaching was to fall.

The seed was sown by visitors from America. Notwithstanding its English name, Keswick spirituality can properly be regarded as a transatlantic import. In the 1830s there had emerged in the United States a new holiness movement. The revivalist Charles Finney and the president of the newly founded Oberlin College, Ohio, Asa Mahan, both came to a crisis of sanctification in 1836. Finney went on to publish *Views on Sanctification* (1840), teaching that human beings had a capacity to fulfil God's command to be perfect. This was the 'Oberlin heresy' of perfectionism. Finney's prestige as a successful evangelist spread his opinions among some of the New School Presbyterians to whom he belonged. The teaching that entire sanctification was available in a personal crisis had broken out of its Methodist confines. Others on the progressive wing of the Reformed tradition took up the theme, sometimes more circumspectly. The crucial text was W. E.

---

[1] C. H. Waller in R. Braithwaite, *The Life and Letters of Rev. William Pennefather*, London, 1878, p. 410.

Boardman's *The Higher Christian Life* (1858). The book urged its readers to move on by faith to a superior form of spirituality. Boardman's title, 'the higher Christian life', became a catchphrase. There was a ripple of interest, but little more, when the book was published in England. Greater fascination arose when Boardman was one of the speakers at Mildmay in 1869; and during the 1870s he became a permanent resident in England. Boardman's personal impact was limited because he lacked the skills of an orator, often turning away from the theme in hand. Yet he played a significant part in making sanctification by faith palatable to Calvinists.

Two other Americans brought the same message but with greater winsomeness: Robert Pearsall Smith and his wife Hannah Whitall Smith. Robert was a Quaker glass manufacturer from Philadelphia, where the traditional piety of the Society of Friends remained stronger than in most parts of England. Original Quaker spirituality was quietist, holding that holiness was to be found through the experience of 'rest' in God. This was to be a significant strand in Keswick teaching. But the Pearsall Smiths had also been subject to Methodist influence. Robert and Hannah had both received the blessing of sanctification through a Methodist holiness camp meeting in 1867. Robert, a man of emotional propensities, was shaken by 'a magnetic thrill of heavenly delight'; Hannah, with a sharper intellect, obtained only what she called a 'knowledge of the truth'.[2] Both started sending papers on their discovery to the English weekly, *The Revival*. Through its pages the message was first widely disseminated in Britain. Robert came over in 1873 and began delivering addresses on holiness by faith. But it was Hannah, with her clear mind and gift for exposition, who made the greater impression. She caused a stir by speaking, although she was a woman, at a private gathering to explore the theme of holiness at Broadlands in Hampshire in 1874. And in the following year she published *The Christian's Secret of a Happy Life*. It was judged to be the most influential book of all in the origins

---

[2] [H.] Pearsall Smith, *The Unselfishness of God and How I Discovered It*, London, 1903, pp. 288, 286.

of Keswick. It seemed sound practical sense, a typical American 'how-to' book by a wife and mother, but written with great perspicuity. The Pearsall Smiths were the effective transmitters of the message across the Atlantic.

A series of meetings between 1873 and 1875 launched the movement. Some of the Mildmay circle were convinced by the idea of sanctification by faith and began to propagate it. One of these was William Haslam, a former High Churchman who had been converted to Evangelical faith (remarkably) by a sermon of his own while he was preaching it. In 1873 he held a small gathering in his Curzon Chapel in London. There, crucially, Evan Hopkins, vicar of Holy Trinity, Richmond, received the blessing. He was to become the chief intellectual formulator of the Keswick tradition down to the First World War. A sequence of annual Broadlands conferences, attended by eclectic groups of church leaders, began in 1874. There were public gatherings over several days at Oxford in 1874 and Brighton in 1875 with Robert Pearsall Smith as the main attraction. During the Brighton meetings came a testing point for the whole venture. Pearsall Smith gave advice to a young woman in a hotel bedroom, foolishly putting his arm round her shoulders. This was undoubtedly a high crime and misdemeanour. Pearsall Smith was sent packing to America and played no further part in the movement. Already, however, plans had been laid for the first convention for the promotion of the spiritual life in the summer of 1875 at Keswick. It became an annual fixture in the calendar. A monthly journal started by Pearsall Smith, *The Christian's Pathway of Power*, was taken over by Evan Hopkins. It was to become, under the new title of *The Life of Faith*, the semi-official periodical of the movement. The Keswick tradition was fairly launched.

How should this form of spirituality be located? It was certainly Evangelical, for the usual quadrilateral is observable. Conversion was a preoccupation of its adherents. Clergy, for instance, were drawn into the movement to secure the spiritual power to preach so that the hearers should undergo the great change. Thus a clergyman went to the Oxford conference because, though crowds attended his ministry on the Isle of Wight, there was 'small result', by which he meant few conversions.[3] The cross was the theological fulcrum of the faith of Keswickers. Hopkins, in a little book called *Hidden Yet Possessed* (1894), warned readers not to be misled by enjoying the resurrection life of consecration. 'We do not say "good-bye" to His crucifixion,' he wrote, 'because we are brought into fellowship with His resurrection.'[4] There was a persistent emphasis on Scripture, with Bible readings, that is, running biblical expositions, a feature of the conventions. We must, affirmed Hopkins, remain 'on the lines of God's written Word'.[5] And those influenced by the movement were notable for their activism. A high Calvinist clergyman, for example, who could not stomach Keswick teaching, nevertheless admitted that its adherents were 'his best workers in the mission hall'.[6] The message of the convention was a great spur to zeal, as its impact on foreign missions from the 1880s was to show. Recruitment for the Church Missionary Society enjoyed a renaissance in that decade when young convention-goers volunteered for service en masse. Keswick fitted firmly within the broader pattern of Evangelicalism.

What is striking, however, is that Keswick had a different atmosphere from the rest of Evangelicalism, whether Reformed or Wesleyan. Both supporters and opponents were aware that it had a distinctive ethos. There are clues to its identification in various details. Mrs Cowper-Temple, for example, the wife of the owner of Broadlands and instigator of the conference there, was a patron of the Pre-Raphaelite Brotherhood of artists. Coleridge was quoted as an authority at the Brighton conference.[7] And Pennefather, the precursor

---

[3] *Account of the Union Meeting for the Promotion of Scriptural Holiness, held at Oxford, August 29 to September 7, 1874*, London, n. d., p. 210 (Rev. Mr Grane, Shanklin).

[4] Evan Hopkins, *Hidden Yet Possessed*, London, 1894, p. 96.

[5] Ibid., pp. 25–6.

[6] I. E. Page, ed., *John Brash: Memorials and Correspondence*, London, 1912, p. 40.

[7] M. E. Dieter, *The Holiness Revival of the Nineteenth Century*, Metuchen, N.J., 1980, pp. 166 n. 37, 180.

of the movement, loved the poetry of Wordsworth.[8] These tastes had not been usual among Evangelicals. Each was a symptom of a feeling for the cultural currents flowing from the Romantic spring. It is clear that the movement was marked in various ways by Romantic affinities.

First, several of those associated with Keswick had poetic inclinations. Thus Frances Ridley Havergal, probably the greatest Evangelical hymnwriter of the nineteenth century, was an adherent of the movement. 'Take my life, and let it be', perhaps her best-known hymn, is a monument of Keswick spirituality. She wrote a great deal of poetry, some of it of considerable quality. 'Thoughts of God', for example, which she thought to be her greatest achievement in verse, contains a memorable image:

> They say there is a hollow, safe and still,
>   A point of coolness and repose
> Within the centre of a flame, where life might dwell
> Unharmed and unconsumed, as in a luminous shell,
>   Which the bright walls of fire enclose
>   In breachless splendour . . .
> So in the centre of these thoughts of God . . .
> *There*, there we find a point of perfect rest
>   And glorious safety.[9]

Like Havergal, Charles Fox, the incumbent of Eaton Chapel, London, was a poet identified with Keswick. A former curate of Pennefather's, Fox shared his former mentor's admiration for Wordsworth. The poetry of the spiritual, Fox believed, was 'one of the most purifying and elevating forces God has given us to lift us to Himself and out of self'.[10] Fox's addresses at Keswick were poetical in tone, even verging on the mystical. Pearsall Smith, who also had a penchant for the mystical,

---

[8] Braithwaite, *Pennefather*, p. 27.
[9] Quoted by J. Grierson, *Frances Ridley Havergal: Worcestershire Hymnwriter*, Bromsgrove, 1979, p. 141.
[10] S. M. Nugent, *Charles Armstrong Fox: Memorials*, London, n. d., p. 210.

attracted criticism for publishing a selection of hymns by F. W. Faber, the Roman Catholic convert from the Oxford Movement, because they revealed 'depth, tenderness, glow, power, and reverential love of God'.[11] Here was a widespread poetical temper that had been rare in the Evangelical world.

Secondly, the Lake District, where the conventions were held, symbolised the appeal of nature for the movement. It was no accident that Keswick was the epicentre. The town had practical advantages. Besides possessing a railway and boarding houses, it was too remote to receive the morning newspapers that might have distracted their readers from higher things. But, more important, the town was in the area so beloved of Wordsworth and Coleridge. The convention leaders shared the poets' love of the natural surroundings, even attributing to them, in Wordsworthian fashion, a moral, educative influence.

> The lovely face of nature's panorama in this valley [ran a report in 1895], if gazed upon with eyes sanctified by thankfulness to God for the gift and the vision to appreciate its charms, must ever have a chastening and purifying effect.[12]

F. B. Meyer, a Baptist minister who was one of the handful of non-Anglicans to achieve prominence in the movement before the First World War, associated his own personal consecration with the forces of nature:

> I rushed out of the tent . . . It was late at night, and the wind was driving the clouds across the lake and past me, and now and again they dropped a few drops on my upturned face . . . 'Father' [he said] 'as I breathe in this breath of the evening air, so I breathe in Thy gift of the Holy Spirit.'[13]

The beauties of the Cumberland scenery were more than pleasant surroundings in which to get away from it all. Rather,

---

[11] *Record*, 24 May 1875.

[12] *Christian*, 25 July 1895, p. 14.

[13] *Keswick Week*, 1920, p. 168. I am grateful to the Rev. Dr Ian Randall for this reference.

nature itself was conceived as a sanctifying force. It was not far short of the pantheism of the early Wordsworth.

There was, thirdly, an element of crisis in Keswick teaching. Dramatic moments were the stock in trade of Romantic literature. The narrow escapes of Scott's narratives were typical of the highly charged juncture, the *kairos*, that compelled attention to Romantic stories. A decisive point of change along these lines was near the centre of the Keswick tradition. At the Oxford conference, Pearsall Smith told his hearers that, 'It is to bring you to a *crisis* of faith that we have come together.' D. B. Hankin, vicar of Christ Church, Ware, echoed him at the same gathering, exhorting the audience to make 'an immediate and complete surrender of self-will and unbelief'.[14] When the Keswick conventions achieved a regular rhythm, day two of the week's programme was devoted to bringing attenders to the stage of consecration. That was not, as Hopkins always insisted, the terminus, but simply the point of departure. Further development in the Christian life was expected afterwards. Handley Moule, later bishop of Durham, the most scholarly exponent of the Keswick position, summed up its message as 'Crisis with a view to a process'.[15] But in that epigram the element of a dramatic turning point remained fundamental.

Faith, fourthly, was exalted by the movement. That holiness came by faith was axiomatic to Keswick. 'It *is* so delicious,' wrote Frances Ridley Havergal, 'to trust him *altogether*.'[16] Hopkins was keen to avert a danger here. 'Don't,' he wrote, 'think of *believing* at all. Think of *Him* who bids you follow Him.'[17] Christ, rather than faith, was to be the object of trust. But the idea of faith was given broad application. At Keswick there was never an appeal for money, even to meet expenses.

---

[14] *Union Meeting . . . at Oxford*, pp. 42, 45.
[15] H. C. Lees, 'The Effect on Individual Ministry', in C. H. Harford, ed., *The Keswick Convention: Its Message, its Method and its Men*, London, 1907, p. 180.
[16] F. R. Havergal to E. H. Hopkins, n. d., in A. Smellie, *Evan Henry Hopkins: A Memoir*, London, 1920, p. 148.
[17] Hopkins, *Hidden Yet Possessed*, p. 21.

Instead, boxes were provided for voluntary offerings. 'It was,' a Keswick sympathiser from America explained, 'a fundamental principle to rest on God for means to carry on His work, rather than look to moneyed men and women.'[18] This was the so-called faith principle that had been recommended by Edward Irving, the irrepressible Church of Scotland minister in London in the 1820s, and had been put into practice by George Müller for his Bristol orphanage and by Hudson Taylor for his China Inland Mission. In each case it was an elevation of faith associated with a downgrading of prudence. That formula marks out the attitude as one kin to the High Church reliance on faith, discussed in chapter one, that emerged from the quixotic atmosphere of Romanticism. Irving, in fact, had derived his inspiration from Coleridge. The faith principle remained in the later nineteenth century as another sign of the Romantic affinities of Keswick.

Notwithstanding the encouragement of activism that has already been noticed, Keswick nurtured, fifthly, an internal sense of peace and relaxation. Hopkins drew a distinction between the 'seeking faith' of the unconsecrated Christian and the 'resting faith' of his consecrated brother. A testimony in *The Christian's Pathway of Power* illustrates the point. According to the writer, his Christian life used to be like 'the bustle of Saturday'. He had 'work and anxiety, with alternations of joy and sorrow'. But since he had let Jesus take entire control of his life, he had enjoyed instead 'peace and rest'.[19] The teaching gave rise at first to exaggeration. Some upheld the notion of 'passive reliance', according to which all human initiative was given up. But by the beginning of the twentieth century this belief was being dismissed as one of the crudities that had disfigured the young movement.[20] Yet the whole ethos of the conventions fostered a sense of calm. The music, for example, was said to be generally 'soft and low'.[21] It was a

[18] A. T. Pierson, *Forward Movements of the Last Half Century*, New York, 1900, p. 44.

[19] *Christian's Pathway of Power*, March 1875, p. 60.

[20] *Record*, 18 January 1901, p. 89 (H. E. Fox).

[21] Smellie, *Hopkins*, p. 178.

far cry from the exuberance of the Methodist tradition, owing more to the peaceful side of Romantic culture.

A sixth feature of the movement was its teaching on the subject (though the word was rarely used) of repression. The fullest statement of the Keswick position came in Evan Hopkins's *The Law of Liberty in the Spiritual Life* (1884). The book distinguished the understanding he represented from the Wesleyan willingness to postulate sinlessness as the result of entire sanctification. Sin was not eradicated, according to Hopkins, but simply repressed. There was sin in the believer until the moment of death, but the Holy Spirit kept the sinful tendencies under control:

> the flesh [wrote Hopkins in another book] is . . . effectively counteracted by . . . the Holy Ghost within us, so that we can walk in the paths of continuous deliverance from it.[22]

The result was victory – for many years a key word in the Keswick vocabulary. So there was a constant struggle going on inside the consecrated believer, but one in which God, if he was allowed, would always defeat the enemies of the soul. It was a typical dynamic concept deriving from a Romantic frame of mind. Consecration did not terminate sin: it inaugurated the ongoing process to which Moule drew attention. Keswick taught repression, not eradication.

The eschatology of the movement, seventhly, was premillennialist. Like the Mildmay conference, Keswick stood for a distinctive position on prophecy. Its adherents believed that Christ would come again before the millennium, so that his return was to be expected very soon. This view was ancient, but it had been revived in the circles around Edward Irving in the early nineteenth century, where it was undoubtedly a sign of a Romantic worldview. The premillennial advent meant that a heroic deliverer was about to appear on the stage of the world to set everything right. Addresses on the advent hope were given at Keswick from its early years. Hopkins believed, according to his biographer, in the personal

---

[22] Hopkins, *Hidden Yet Possessed*, p. 63.

advent, the rapture of the saints and the imminence of the consummation.[23] Prebendary H. W. Webb-Peploe, a staunch Keswick protagonist, urged that perhaps within his lifetime, 'the Master may be seen in the clouds of heaven, gathering his own elect unto Himself'.[24] A Methodist minister, on the other hand, who was recruited to speak at subsidiary conventions on Keswick lines, was once asked by the organiser to give an address on the Lord's coming. The minister replied that he did not belong to the organiser's school of thought; and the man was struck dumb.[25] Keswick's premillennialism differed entirely from the broadening postmillennial perspective of the Wesleyan tradition. Here was a doctrinal position, Romantic in its associations, that marked off Keswick from many others.

The prevailing attitude to doctrine in the Keswick movement, however, was originally far less definite than its teaching about the second coming. J. C. Ryle, soon the Evangelical bishop of Liverpool, criticised convention-goers in 1878 for their dislike of dogma.[26] The charge was not unfair. Pearsall Smith had written that tender souls were kept back from the way of holiness by 'the death-clothes of doctrine'.[27] Apart from a Quaker tendency not to stress doctrinal precision, Pearsall Smith had a powerful motive for playing down dogma in his desire to bring together Calvinists and Arminians. In holiness meetings, he said, the two parties found themselves less different than they had supposed.[28] Likewise T. D. Harford-Battersby, the Keswick clergyman who convened the gatherings, included in his first invitation a deprecation of 'the hard, dry lines of scientific theology'.[29] The consequence was that the early movement showed more doctrinal latitude than might be expected of Evangelicals. Hannah Whitall Smith, for example, was allowed to speak at

---

[23] Smellie, *Hopkins*, p. 207.
[24] *Record*, 18 January 1901, p. 99.
[25] I. E. Page, ed., *Brash*, p. 178.
[26] *Record*, 21 January 1878.
[27] *Revival*, 3 December 1868, p. 672.
[28] *Christian*, 5 March 1874.
[29] *Record*, 14 June 1875.

Broadlands although some knew in advance that she was a universalist.[30] Many in and around the first few Keswicks had an attitude to doctrine that was closer to that of Broad Churchmen than to that typical of Evangelicals. The Cowper-Temples, in fact, the hosts at Broadlands, would normally be classed as Broad Church. The reason for these affinities was that the Romantic influences eroding the sharp contours of doctrine among Broad Churchmen were also having an effect on Keswick.

A hallmark of new nineteenth-century patterns of thought, developing in the wake of the Romantic movement, was cultural relativism. Each society, on this view, has its own standards which are as valid as those of any other. This notion is called in Germany *Historismus*, the intellectual assumption that values are generated by their social context and relate to that context only. It was a wave of thinking that in the later nineteenth century began to affect theory in many areas such as economics and anthropology. Facets of this style of thinking are evident around Keswick. Faith, according to an article of 1868 by Pearsall Smith, gave power of overcoming all *discerned* sin. At one level this was merely a restatement of Wesley's teaching that entire sanctification entailed the absence of all known sin. But in Pearsall Smith's understanding it had wider implications:

> A heathen converted last week may now be walking up to the standard to which he has 'already attained', and yet be in practices from which a further knowledge of God's will shall separate him. Through all the steps of his advance, he may, through Christ, have no stain on his conscience (or knowledge).[31]

This perfection, Pearsall Smith explained, was Christian, not divine – by which he meant relative, not absolute. There was a legitimate difference between the moral rule in one society and its equivalent in another. This was certainly a break with traditional Christian ethics, according to which anything that

---

[30] [H.] Pearsall Smith, *Unselfishness of God*, p. 223.
[31] *Revival*, 10 December 1868, p. 683.

was wrong was so in all circumstances. It is remarkable that a holiness movement should be teaching what from the most obvious point of view was a laxer form of morality. But that paradoxical conclusion was a corollary of the historical relativism of the times. Here was a further symptom of the rise of the Keswick tradition being bound up with Romantic cultural attitudes.

It is not surprising that the Keswick movement, so different from Evangelical norms in so many ways, attracted censure from other Evangelicals. It was criticised from the standpoint of the Wesleyan tradition. For Methodists, the movement was altogether too Calvinist. Few Methodists appeared on its platform, the only one to attain prominence before the First World War being the Irishman Charles Inwood. 'There can be no agreement,' commented the Wesleyan holiness leader John Brash, 'so long as there are Arminians and Calvinists.'[32] The disagreement was dramatised at the Brighton conference. Brash told the members of the audience that if they were in a certain condition, they needed to ask if they were Christians at all. Sin, he was assuming, prevented a person from being in a right relationship with God. The next speaker, however, was Evan Hopkins, who, from the Reformed standpoint, reassured the listeners. They might have lapsed into sins, he told them, but they were still justified by Christ. Their state might be sinful, but their standing as Christians was secure.[33] The distinction between state and standing was simply unacceptable to Methodists. To the Anglicans who dominated Keswick, however, it was fundamental, because it was the only way to ensure that assurance of salvation was not lost. Here was the first reason why most Methodists stood apart from Keswick.

The second reason arose from the question of eradication. Methodists, as we noted in the last chapter, generally believed in the possibility of sin being rooted out of a human life. Keswick, as we have already seen in this one, believed it was

---

[32] Page, ed., *Brash*, p. 34.

[33] Ibid., p. 35. Hopkins must surely be the individual identified as H_____ .

merely being repressed. Hopkins took pains to guard the new movement against the charge of teaching sinlessness. The conventions, Meyer declared in 1892, did not hold that 'the flesh' was extracted from the believer. He dismissed any such 'mechanical theory'.[34] Three years later there was a well publicised episode when Reader Harris of the Pentecostal League of Prayer issued a challenge. He would give £100 to anyone who could prove from Scripture that sin must remain in the believer. Nobody, needless to say, responded to his satisfaction. Harris represented the Wesleyan tradition; the target of his attack was Keswick. It was essentially a clash between two cultural idioms, the 'mechanical' vocabulary of the Enlightenment against the organic language of Romanticism. But the effect was to maintain the gulf between the Wesleyan and the Keswick stances.

Keswick was criticised more widely and more sharply from the standpoint of the Reformed tradition. For Calvinists, the movement was too Arminian. For one thing, it seemed to teach perfectionism. When, in the 1870s, Webb-Peploe addressed a group of Evangelical clergy on the new teaching, the chairman reacted sharply: 'Heresy!' he cried, 'Heresy!! Damnable heresy! I hold it is for the glory of God that we should fall into sin, that He may get honour to Himself by drawing us out of it!'[35] There was no escaping sin in this mortal life. The Rev. Sir Emilius Bayley was another outspoken critic of the developments leading to Keswick. But his worldview was built on 'the Moral Government of God', on science, on 'well attested facts'.[36] This was the language of an older generation schooled in Enlightenment categories. Once more there was a cultural as well as a theological difference between Keswick and its critics.

The same was true of a further main feature of the Calvinist critique of Keswick. It was the claim that faith was not a valid path to holiness. The charge was laid by Spurgeon. Some, he

---

[34] *Christian*, 4 August 1892, p. 8.
[35] Evan Hopkins, 'Preliminary Stages' in Harford, ed., *Keswick Convention*, pp. 39–40.
[36] *Record*, 19 February 1875; 18 January 1882.

asserted in 1873, 'have the notion that they have overcome all their sins by believing that they have done so'. What they termed faith, Spurgeon, who rarely minced words, called 'a lazy, self-conceited presumption'.[37] It was an avoidance of the battle against sin that must always occupy the Christian life. J. C. Ryle's much reissued *Holiness* (1877), a sustained polemic against Keswick, expressed similar reservations. Is it wise, he asks, 'to speak of faith as the one thing needful'? Surely, he continues, 'the Scriptures teach us that in following holiness the true Christian needs personal exertion and work as well as faith'.[38] These Calvinist opponents were fearful of the old spectre of antinomianism. If the conflict against unrighteousness were not kept up, then people would fall into wrongdoing. The critics did not share the enlarged concept of faith of the Keswickers. For the convention-goers, faith was always sufficient to guarantee victory over sin. It was the Romantic style of faith that meant total dependence on God and, in the last resort, the power of the Almighty himself. To that understanding of faith neither Spurgeon nor Ryle gave his allegiance.

The same cultural clash also marked the final chief disagreement between the Reformed camp and Keswick. Calvinist critics feared that the crisis of which Pearsall Smith and his successors spoke was a spurious substitute for a steady advance in the Christian life. G. T. Fox wrote that God the Father 'is glorified not in the instantaneous perfection of his redeemed, but in their gradual deliverance from imperfection'.[39] Spurgeon thought similarly. 'The condition,' he declared, 'in which a believer should always be found is progress: his motto must be, "Onward and upward!"'[40] These Calvinists were standing for the gradualism of their tradition that went back for centuries. But their position was reinforced by the meliorism of the high Victorian period, associated with such

---

[37] C. H. Spurgeon, 'Onward!' (25 May 1873), *Twelve Sermons on Sanctification*, London, n. d., p. 286.

[38] J. C. Ryle, *Holiness*, London, 1887, pp. i, ii.

[39] *Record*, 18 June 1875.

[40] C. H. Spurgeon, 'Onward!', p. 273.

popular writers as Samuel Smiles, that harked back to the optimism of the Enlightenment. Hard work, on this view, would reap its reward. The unreconstructed Calvinists had a strong suspicion of any suggestion that there was a short cut to anything worth achieving, least of all to holiness. The notion of leaping at once to a 'higher life' seemed entirely alien. Spirituality was a battleground between contrasting cultural styles.

The newer mode was more attractive to the educated, the prosperous and the young. That is why Keswick specially drew in university undergraduates, whose presence in large numbers was a regular feature of the conventions. The Lakeland gathering was very much an elite affair. Only those with a week's leisure, still a rare attribute in the late nineteenth century, could attend at all. A friendly critic voiced the fear in 1895 that the convention was becoming an event for the rich alone.[41] Inwood once remarked that he supposed his hearers must be wearing jewellery worth at least £10,000.[42] Because it appealed to the elite, the denominational balance was skewed. Few Nonconformists attended, and fewer spoke. Anglicans, with their disproportionate representation among the educated and the prosperous, dominated the movement. Pearsall Smith was well suited to this constituency. He was, according to a Methodist observer, 'a man of prepossessing appearance, sweetness of spirit and suavity of manner, exactly adapted to his work among the well-to-do, especially of the Anglican Church.'[43] Keswick was well integrated with the establishment, social and ecclesiastical.

The new teaching on sanctification by faith steadily disarmed the fears of its critics. Its progress can be monitored at the Islington Clerical Conference, the annual jamboree of the Evangelical Anglicans. In the later nineteenth century, when the topic of holiness came under discussion, there was a main paper followed by wider discussion. In 1889, the first

---

[41] J. C. Pollock, *The Keswick Story*, London, 1964, p. 111.
[42] *Keswick Week*, 1909, p. 239. Again I am grateful to the Rev. Dr Ian Randall for this reference.
[43] Page, ed., *Brash*, p. 153.

address was still hostile to Keswick, with only a subordinate second speech in favour. Three years later, however, the first speaker was favourable, with criticism coming only after-wards from the floor. By 1901, when the previous century was reviewed, there was only one speaker on 'Holiness of Life', and he represented Keswick.[44] The new movement had won the allegiance of the Evangelical party in the Church of England. Five years later the convention was said to be attracting as many as 10,000 people.[45] There were to be troubles just after the First World War when some advanced liberal Evangelicals put forward views that were outright pantheism. The crisis was surmounted, however, and the convention was consolidated as the backbone of twentieth-century conservative Evangelicalism. Its continuing associa-tion with the young meant that it became the seedbed of the Inter-Varsity Fellowship that was to transform the face of Christianity in England and beyond in the later twentieth cen-tury. The distinctive message of holiness by faith was to fade away in the 1960s, with the convention continuing as a vehicle for high-level biblical exposition. But in its day Keswick had caught the spirit of the age. Its heroic but restful spirituality, reflecting the advancing Romantic mood of the times, remoulded the English Evangelical movement.

---

[44] *Record*, 18 January 1889, pp. 55–6; 15 January 1892, pp. 69–71; 18 January 1901, pp. 88–9.
[45] Harford, *Keswick Convention*, p. 15.

Conclusion

Three overall inferences can be drawn from this survey. First, it can be affirmed that holiness is an important theme for historical research in the nineteenth as in previous centuries. Undoubtedly the quality of life displayed by many of the individuals touched upon here exerted a major influence over others. Pusey by his wholehearted ascetic practice drew hundreds of undergraduates to him for wise counsel. Spurgeon's sermons, with their vast worldwide circulation, prompted many to greater dedication. Keswick speakers roused dozens, often at a single meeting, to travel to distant lands as heralds of the gospel. It is no wonder that there should be these consequences, for sanctity, in whatever form, has its own appeal. A good instance is John Rattenbury, a Wesleyan exponent of full salvation in the mid-nineteenth century:

> He was a holy man, sanctity was essentially wrought into his being, it pervaded his speech, sat on his countenance, dominated his life; he 'walked with God' in elevated and habitual companionship. Herein lay the secret of his marvellous power in prayer and preaching . . .[1]

There was nothing starchy about Rattenbury: in ordinary conversation he could be quick in repartee – but there was no sting in his remarks. The impact of the man was undeniable:

> I heard him [wrote a fellow-minister] in the Centenary Chapel in York preach on the subject of 'Purity of Heart and Life', when the mighty congregation was moved sometimes to tears, and

---

[1] J. D. Tetley, 'Recollections of his Ministry in York', in H. O. Rattenbury, ed., *The Rev. John Rattenbury: Memorials*, London, 1884, p. 96.

sometimes to loudest bursts of pent-up feeling, and many entered into the privilege of the sons of God.[2]

Scarcely any contemporary was a more effective evangelist. John Rattenbury must have been the reason why thousands went to chapel. The secondary literature has rightly examined the reasons why the mass of the people did or did not go to places of worship in the nineteenth century. They might attend in order to achieve respectability or to qualify for the rites of passage; they might not join in worship because they were too poor to pay pew rents or because they preferred the public house. All these social factors – and more – did operate. Yet so did sanctity. Those who claimed to know the way to heaven exhorted others to worship its king. It helped if they reflected his character as they spoke. The power of holiness to attract the people to church needs to be integrated into the secondary literature.

Secondly, holiness interacts with its cultural environment. Understandings of spirituality were shaped in part by preconceptions current at the time. Some supposed sanctification to be a matter of individual progress. Their general optimism led them to anticipate that believers would make advances in the Christian life, but the improvement, if persevered in, was expected to be gradual and steady. They were indebted to the Enlightenment for this idea of progress. Others thought sanctification to be possible only in the community of the church. Nourished by its sacraments and sustained by its worship, they would be numbered among the saved if their spiritual habits fitted them for heaven. Their feelings were expressed in a Romantic idiom. Such movements have sometimes been treated in theological isolation, as though holiness were a matter of doctrine alone. Certainly spirituality is shaped by theology; but it is also affected by social practices and, on the evidence presented here, by other ideas current at any given time. The Enlightenment and Romanticism, as these chapters have tried to show, generated ways of thinking that

---

[2]   G. Smith, 'Memorial Sketch', in ibid., p. 45.

helped shape nineteenth-century patterns of holiness. They enriched believers' awareness of themes in Scripture and in the religious traditions they had received. Equally these non-theological considerations complicated theological debate. Controversy was often as much about contemporary packaging as about doctrinal substance. Consequently the different versions of holiness can be appreciated only in their cultural settings.

Thirdly, nineteenth-century patterns of spirituality were formative for the century that was to follow. The masses of the nineteenth century were far more affected by the Enlightenment of the eighteenth century than by the Romanticism that succeeded it. The popular forms of devotional practice were therefore those with Enlightenment overtones: the Calvinist tradition in its moderate, Fullerite expression and the Wesleyan tradition in the shape inherited from Wesley himself. Insofar as either was modified, initially it was further in the direction of Enlightenment values. There was an erosion of the distinctiveness of Calvinism and Wesleyanism and there followed a consolidation of a common Evangelical ethos. The nineteenth century, however, gave rise to new cultural currents associated with the Romantic movement. These novelties appealed to the elite, to those people who were aware of the fresh developments and had the leisure to pursue them. Thus the upper classes and the upper middle classes were drawn to new forms of piety: the revitalised High Church tradition in the Church of England and the Keswick tradition in the Evangelical movement. These were what satisfied the spiritual aspirations of those who formed opinion for the future. Hence these were the species of devotion that spread outwards geographically and down the social scale as time went on. There were increasing numbers of High Churchmen indebted to the Oxford Movement and of Keswickers attending the conventions at the turn of the twentieth century. The Calvinist and Wesleyan traditions, still largely reliant on older styles of cultural expression, went into eclipse in the twentieth century, though there was to be a revival of Reformed teaching in its second half. But roughly down to the 1960s the High Church party dominated the Church of

England and Keswick dominated the Evangelical movement. If the cultural forms of the nineteenth century underlie the ecclesiastical patterns of the following century, it is to their equivalent in the twentieth century that we must turn in order to discern the likely developments in the English churches during the twenty-first century.

Further Reading

This list is confined to published works and, in the main, to readily accessible books. After a few general items, it is organised according to the chapter structure of this book.

General

O. Chadwick, *The Victorian Church*, 2 vols, London, 1966, 1970.

H. Davies, *Worship and Theology in England*, Princeton, N.J., vol. 3, *From Watts and Wesley to Maurice, 1690–1850*, 1961; vol. 4, *From Newman to Martineau, 1850–1900*, 1962.

J. M. Gordon, *Evangelical Spirituality*, London, 1991.

M. Heimann, *Catholic Devotion in Victorian England*, Oxford, 1995.

I. Randall, *Evangelical Experiences: A Study in the Spirituality of English Evangelicalism, 1918–1939*, Carlisle, 1999.

1. The High Church Tradition

J. Bentley, *Ritualism and Politics in Victorian Britain: The Attempt to Legislate for Belief*, Oxford, 1978.

P. Butler, ed., *Pusey Rediscovered*, London, 1983.

O. Chadwick, *The Mind of the Oxford Movement*, London, 1960. Contains illustrative documents.

O. Chadwick, *The Spirit of the Oxford Movement*, London, 1990. Collection of essays.

S. Gilley, *Newman and his Age*, London, 1990.

A. Härdelin, *The Tractarian Understanding of the Eucharist*, Uppsala, 1965.

I. Ker, *John Henry Newman: A Biography*, Oxford, 1988.

P. B. Nockles, *The Oxford Movement in Context: Anglican High Churchmanship, 1760–1857*, Cambridge, 1994.

W. S. F. Pickering, *Anglo-Catholicism: A Study in Religious Ambiguity*, London, 1989.

G. Rowell, *The Vision Glorious: Themes and Personalities of the Catholic Revival in Anglicanism*, Oxford, 1983.

2. The Calvinist Tradition

D. W. Bebbington, *Evangelical Conversion, c.1740–1850*, North Atlantic Missiology Project Position Paper 21, Cambridge, 1997.

D. W. Bebbington, *Evangelicalism in Modern Britain: A History from the 1730s to the 1980s*, London, 1989. Chapters 1 and 2.

D. W. Bebbington, *Victorian Nonconformity*, Bangor, Gwynedd, 1992.

B. Hilton, *The Age of Atonement: The Influence of Evangelicalism on Social and Economic Thought, 1785–1865*, Oxford, 1988.

B. Hindmarsh, *John Newton and the English Evangelical Tradition: Between the Conversions of Wesley and Wilberforce*, Oxford, 1996.

K. Hylson-Smith, *Evangelicals in the Church of England, 1734–1984*, Edinburgh, 1989.

P. S. Kruppa, *Charles Haddon Spurgeon: A Preacher's Progress*, New York, 1982.

M. L. Loane, *John Charles Ryle, 1816–1900*, London, 1983.

D. W. Lovegrove, *Established Church, Sectarian People: Itinerancy and the Transformation of English Dissent, 1780–1830*, Cambridge, 1988.

P. Toon, *Evangelical Theology, 1833–1856: A Response to Tractarianism*, Basingstoke, 1983.

3. The Wesleyan Tradition

D. W. Bebbington, 'Holiness in Nineteeenth-Century British Methodism', in W. M. Jacob and N. Yates, ed., *Crown and Mitre: Religion and Society in Northern Europe since the Reformation*, Woodbridge, Suffolk, 1993.

D. W. Bebbington, 'The Holiness Movements in British and Canadian Methodism in the Late Nineteenth Century', *Proceedings of the Wesley Historical Society*, 50, 1996.

R. Carwardine, *Transatlantic Revivalism: Popular Evangelicalism in Britain and America, 1790–1865*, Westport, Conn., 1978.

J. Kent, *Holding the Fort: Studies in Victorian Revivalism*, London, 1978.

H. Lindström, *Wesley and Sanctification: A Study in the Doctrine of Salvation*, London, n. d.

D. M. Valenze, *Prophetic Sons and Daughters: Female Preaching and Popular Religion in Industrial England*, Princeton, N.J., 1985.

G. S. Wakefield, *Methodist Devotion: The Spiritual Life in the Methodist Tradition*, London, 1966.

4. The Keswick Tradition

D. W. Bebbington, *Evangelicalism in Modern Britain: A History from the 1730s to the 1980s*, London, 1989. Chapter 5.

M. Dieter, *The Holiness Revival of the Nineteenth Century*, Metuchen, N.J., 1980.

J. C. Pollock, *The Keswick Story*, London, 1964.

I. Randall, *Pathway of Power: Keswick and the Reshaping of Wesleyan Holiness, 1875–1905*, Shearsby, near Lutterworth, Leicestershire, 1999.

The Didsbury Lectures

(published by Paternoster Press unless otherwise stated)

1996   R. Bauckham
        **God Crucified: Monotheism and Christology in the
        New Testament**
1997   H.G.M. Williamson
        **Variations on a Theme: King, Messiah and Servant in the
        Book of Isaiah**
1998   D. Bebbington
        Holiness in Nineteenth-Century England
1999   L.W. Hurtado
        At the Origins of Christian Worship
2000   C. Pinnock
        The Most Moved Mover
        (forthcoming)

*   no longer available
†   not published
††   not part of the Paternoster Didsbury series